Best of Nancy Rink Quilts

9 Classic Quilts from Timeless Blocks

Contents

Nine-Patch Rails

Finished Quilt Size: 92" x 92" (234 cm x 234 cm)
Finished Block Size: 4½" x 4½" (11 cm x 11 cm)

Quilted by Eve Hall

In Nancy's quilt, the Nine-Patch Blocks are scrappy. Some of the pieces in each block match, others of the pieces in each block match, others don't. Feel free to mix and match your scraps as Nancy did.

SHOPPING LIST

Yardage is based on 43"/44" (109 cm/112 cm) wide fabric with a usable width of 40" (102 cm).

- ☐ 3½ - 3¾ yds (3.2 m - 3.4 m) **total** of assorted light print fabrics
- ☐ 2¾ - 3 yds (2.5 m - 2.7 m) **total** of assorted medium and dark print fabrics
- ☐ ⅞ yd (80 cm) of red tone-on-tone fabric for setting triangles
- ☐ ⅝ yd (57 cm) of beige print fabric for inner border
- ☐ 2¾ yds (2.5 m) of red print fabric for outer border
- ☐ ⅞ yd (80 cm) of fabric for binding
- ☐ 8½ yds (7.8 m) of fabric for backing
- ☐ 100" x 100" (254 cm x 254 cm) piece of batting

CUTTING THE PIECES

*Follow **Rotary Cutting,** page 55, to cut fabric. Cut all strips from the selvage-to-selvage width of the fabric unless otherwise stated. Outer borders are cut longer than needed and will be trimmed to fit quilt top center. All measurements include ¼" seam allowances.*

From assorted light print fabrics:

- Cut 288 **rectangles A** 2" x 5".
- Cut 484 **squares B** 2" x 2".

From assorted medium and dark print fabrics:

- Cut 144 **rectangles A** 2" x 5".
- Cut 605 **squares B** 2" x 2".

From red tone-on-tone fabric:

- Cut 3 strips 7¾" wide. From these strips, cut 11 squares 7¾" x 7¾". Cut each square **twice** diagonally to make **44 triangles C.***
- Cut 1 strip 4½" wide. From this strip, cut 2 squares 4½" x 4½". Cut each square **once** diagonally to make 4 **triangles D.***

From beige print fabric:

- Cut 9 **inner border strips** 2" wide.

From red print fabric:

- Cut 2 lengthwise **outer side borders** 6½" x 83½".
- Cut 2 lengthwise **outer top/bottom borders** 6½" x 95½".

From binding fabric:

- Cut 11 **binding strips** 2¼" **wide.**

***These pieces are cut slightly oversized to allow for trimming after construction.**

MAKING THE RAIL BLOCKS

*Follow **Machine Piecing**, page 56, and **Pressing**, page 57, to make quilt top. Use ¼" **seam allowances throughout**.*

1. Sew together two light print **rectangles A** and one medium or dark print **rectangle A** to make a **Rail Block**. Press the seam allowances toward the medium or dark print fabric. Make 144 Rail Blocks.

Rail Block (make 144)

MAKING THE NINE PATCH BLOCKS

1. Sew together four light print **squares B** and five medium or dark print **squares B** to make a **Nine Patch Block**. Sew the squares together in rows, pressing the seam allowances toward the darker fabric. Sew the rows together. Make 121 Nine Patch Blocks.

Nine Patch Block (make 121)

ASSEMBLING THE QUILT TOP

Refer to **Quilt Top** to assemble quilt top.

1. Alternating the Blocks, sew the Blocks and **triangle C's** together in diagonal rows. Sew the rows together.
2. Sew a **triangle D** to each corner.
3. Trim the quilt top to measure 76½" x 76½".
4. Using diagonal seams, sew **inner border strips** together to make one continuous strip ***(Fig. 1)***.

Fig. 1

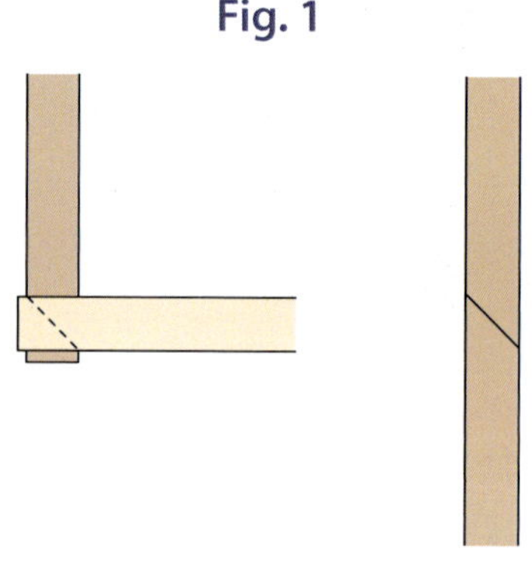

5. Measure *length* across center of quilt top center. Cut 2 **inner side borders** from continuous strip. Matching centers and corners, sew inner side borders to quilt top center.
6. Measure *width* across center of quilt top center (including added borders). Cut 2 **inner top/bottom borders** from continuous strip. Matching centers and corners, sew inner top/bottom borders to quilt top center.
7. Repeat Steps 5-6 to add **outer top/bottom**, then **outer side borders**.

QUILT TOP

COMPLETING THE QUILT

1. Follow **Quilting,** page 63, to mark, layer, and quilt as desired. Quilt shown is quilted with all-over meandering design.

2. Follow **Making a Hanging Sleeve,** page 65, if a hanging sleeve is desired.

3. Sew **binding strips** together end to end diagonally. Follow **Attaching Binding with Mitered Corners,** page 66, to bind quilt.

Quilt Top Diagram

American Pastimes

Finished Quilt Size: 65" x 85" (165 cm x 216 cm)
Finished Block Size: 10" x 10" (25 cm x 25 cm)

SHOPPING LIST

Yardage is based on 43"/44" (109 cm/112 cm) wide fabric with a usable width of 40" (102 cm).

- ☐ ⅝ yd (57 cm) ***each*** of 3 assorted red print fabrics
- ☐ ⅝ yd (57 cm) ***each*** of 5 assorted blue print fabrics
- ☐ ⅝ yd (57 cm) of tan print fabric
- ☐ ⅝ yd (57 cm) of brown print fabric
- ☐ ⅞ yd (80 cm) ***each*** of 4 assorted cream print fabrics
- ☐ ⅞ yd (80 cm) of cream novelty print fabric (Ours features baseball players.)
- ☐ 1⅜ yds (1.3 m) of red and blue stripe fabric for inner borders and binding
- ☐ 5¼ yds (4.8 m) of fabric for backing

You will also need:

- ☐ 73" x 93" (185 cm x 236 cm) piece of batting
- ☐ 68 sheets of That Patchwork Place® 8½" x 11" (22 cm x 28 cm) papers for foundation piecing

CUTTING THE PIECES

*Follow **Rotary Cutting**, page 55, to cut fabric. Cut all strips across the selvage-to-selvage width of the fabric. Inner Borders include extra length for "insurance" and will be trimmed after assembling quilt top center.*
All measurements include ¼" seam allowances.

From red print #1 fabric:

- Cut 1 strip 2½"w. From this strip, cut 15 **squares A** 2½" x 2½".
- Cut 3 strips 3"w. From these strips, cut 29 **squares B** 3" x 3".

From red print #2 fabric:

- Cut 2 strips 2½"w. From these strips, cut 24 **squares A** 2½" x 2½".
- Cut 2 strips 2"w for paper pieced diamond block.
- Cut 1 strip 3¼"w. From this strip, cut 5 squares 3¼" x 3¼". Cut each square ***once*** diagonally to make 10 **triangles A2.**

From red print #3 fabric:

- Cut 1 strip 2½"w. From this strip, cut 15 **squares A** 2½" x 2½".
- Cut 1 strip 3"w. From this strip, cut 12 **squares B** 3" x 3".

From blue print #1 fabric:

- Cut 1 strip 2½"w. From this strip, cut 15 **squares A** 2½" x 2½".
- Cut 3 strips 3"w. From these strips, cut 29 **squares B** 3" x 3".

From blue print #2 fabric:

- Cut 2 strips 2½"w. From these strips, cut 24 **squares A** 2½" x 2½".
- Cut 2 strips 2"w for paper pieced diamond block.
- Cut 1 strip 3¼"w. From this strip, cut 5 squares 3¼" x 3¼". Cut each square ***once*** diagonally to make 10 **triangles A2.**

From blue print #3 fabric:

- Cut 1 strip 2½"w. From this strip, cut 15 **squares A** 2½" x 2½".
- Cut 1 strip 3"w. From this strip, cut 12 **squares B** 3" x 3".
- Cut 2 strips 2"w for paper pieced diamond block.
- Cut 1 strip 3¼"w. From this strip, cut 5 squares 3¼" x 3¼". Cut each square ***once*** diagonally to make 10 **triangles A2.**

From blue print #4 fabric:

- Cut 1 strip 2½"w. From this strip, cut 15 **squares A** 2½" x 2½".
- Cut 1 strip 3"w. From this strip, cut 12 **squares B** 3" x 3".
- Cut 2 strips 2"w for paper pieced diamond block.
- Cut 1 strip 3¼"w. From this strip, cut 5 squares 3¼" x 3¼". Cut each square ***once*** diagonally to make 10 **triangles A2.**

From blue print #5 fabric:

- Cut 2 strips 2"w for paper pieced diamond block.
- Cut 1 strip 3¼"w. From this strip, cut 5 squares 3¼" x 3¼". Cut each square ***once*** diagonally to make 10 **triangles A2.**

From tan print fabric:

- Cut 2 strips 2½"w. From these strips, cut 24 **squares A** 2½" x 2½".
- Cut 2 strips 2"w for paper pieced diamond block.
- Cut 1 strip 3¼"w. From this strip, cut 5 squares 3¼" x 3¼c". Cut each square ***once*** diagonally to make 10 **triangles A2.**

From brown print fabric:

- Cut 1 strip 2½"w. From this strip, cut 15 **squares A** 2½" x 2½".
- Cut 1 strip 3"w. From this strip, cut 12 **squares B** 3" x 3".
- Cut 2 strips 2"w for paper pieced diamond block.
- Cut 1 strip 3¼"w. From this strip, cut 5 squares 3¼" x 3¼". Cut each square ***once*** diagonally to make 10 **triangles A2**

From *each* of 3 cream print fabrics:

- Cut 2 strips 2½"w. From these strips, cut 24 **squares A** 2½" x 2½".
- Cut 2 strips 3"w. From these strips, cut 24 **squares B** 3" x 3".
- Cut 3 strips 2"w for paper pieced diamond block.
- Cut 4 strips 2¾"w for paper pieced diamond block.

From cream #4 print fabric:

- Cut 5 strips 2½"w. From these strips, cut 18 **squares A** 2½" x 2½" and 18 **rectangles C** 2½" x 6½".
- Cut 2 strips 2"w for paper pieced diamond block.
- Cut 4 strips 2¾"w for paper pieced diamond block.

From cream novelty print fabric:

- Cut 5 strips 2½"w. From these strips, cut 18 **squares A** 2½" x 2½" and 18 **rectangles C** 2½" x 6½".
- Cut 2 strips 2"w for paper pieced diamond block.
- Cut 4 strips 2¾"w for paper pieced diamond block.

From red and blue stripe fabric:

- Cut 2 strips 2"w for paper pieced diamond block.
- Cut 7 strips 2½"w. Sew strips together end to end and recut into 2 top/bottom inner borders 2½" x 58½" and 2 side inner borders 2½" x 74½".
- Cut 9 binding strips 2¼"w.

From remaining assorted color print fabrics:

- Cut 132 **rectangles D** 2½" x 5½".
- Cut 4 **squares E** 3½" x 3½".
- Cut 4 **rectangles F** 2½" x 3½.

ASSEMBLING THE BLOCKS

These blocks should be very scrappy. Feel free to randomly mix and match the various strips and triangles. The cutting instructions included extra pieces to allow for freedom in the fabric placement.

DIAMOND BLOCKS

1. Photocopy ¼ **Diamond Block** pattern, page 13, onto foundation piecing paper. Make 68 photocopies.

2. Choose 17 red print #1 and 17 blue print #1 **squares B**. Cut each square ***once*** diagonally to make 34 red triangles and 34 blue triangles for position A5.

3. Referring to pattern for fabric placement and trimming strips as needed, refer to **Foundation Paper Piecing,** page 56, to stitch and flip strips and triangles in numerical order beginning in the A1 position.

4. Sew 4 of the paper pieced ¼ **Diamond Blocks** together to make a **Diamond Block**, making sure A5 triangles are placed in the center. Press seam allowances open. Make 17 **Diamond Blocks**.

Diamond Block (make 17)

STAR BLOCKS

*Follow **Machine Piecing,** page 56, and **Pressing,** page 57.*
Use a ¼" seam allowance for piecing.

1. Choose 4 **squares A** and 4 **squares B** from 1 cream print, 5 **squares A** and 4 **squares B** from 1 red print, 4 **squares A** from 1 blue print, and 2 **squares A** and 2 **rectangles C** from cream novelty print.

2. Sew 2 cream novelty print **squares A**, and 1 red print **square A** together to make Unit 1. Press seam allowances toward red print square.

3. Draw a diagonal line on the wrong side of 4 red print **squares A**. Matching right sides, place red print squares on ends of 2 cream novelty print **rectangles C** as shown in ***Fig. 1***.

4. Sew each square along drawn lines. Trim ¼" from drawn line as shown in ***Fig. 2*** and press open to make 2 Unit 2's.

5. Draw a diagonal line on the wrong side of 1 cream print **square B**. Matching right sides, place cream print square (B) on top of 1 red print **square B**. Stitch ¼" from each side of drawn line ***(Fig. 3)***. Cut along drawn line; press open, pressing seam allowances toward the red print fabric to make 2 Unit 3's. Make 8 Unit 3's. Trim each Unit 3 to 2½" x 2½".

6. Referring to **Star Block Diagram**, sew 1 Unit 1, 2 Unit 2's, 8 Unit 3's, 4 cream print **squares A**, and 4 blue print **squares A** together to make Star Block. Repeat Steps 1-6 to make a total of 3 Star Blocks in this color way.

7. Refer to **Additional Star Block Diagrams** and repeat Steps 2-6 to make 3 Star Blocks of each color way to make a total of 18 Star Blocks.

Unit 1

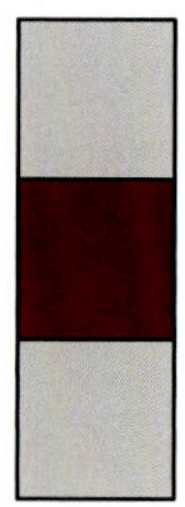

Fig. 1

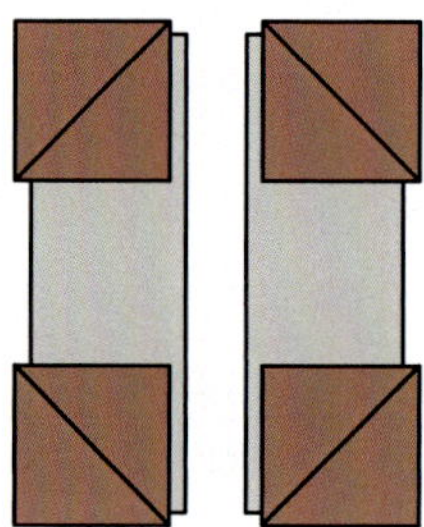

Fig. 2

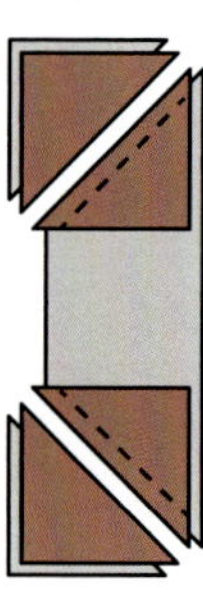

Unit 2

Fig. 3

Unit 3 (make 8)

ASSEMBLING THE QUILT TOP CENTER

Refer to ***Quilt Top Diagram,*** *page 12, for assembly.*

1. Beginning with a Star Block and alternating blocks, sew 3 Star Blocks and 2 Diamond Blocks together to make Row 1. Make 4 Row 1's.

2. Beginning with a Diamond Block and alternating blocks, sew 3 Diamond Blocks and 2 Star Blocks together to make Row 2. Make 3 Row 2's.

3. Sew Rows 1 and 2 together to make Quilt Top Center.

ADDING THE BORDERS

1. Refer to **Adding Squared Borders,** page 62, to add side, then top and bottom inner borders to quilt top center.

2. Sew 1 **rectangle D**, 1 **square E**, and 1 **rectangle F** together to make Border Corner. Make 4 Border Corners.

3. Randomly sew together 37 **rectangles D** to make Side Outer Border. Make 2 Side Outer Borders.

4. Sew 1 Side Outer Border to each side of quilt top. It may be necessary to make border seams wider or narrower to adjust the length to fit the quilt top.

5. Randomly sew together 27 **rectangles D** to make Top Outer Border. Repeat to make Bottom Outer Border.

6. Noting orientation of **Border Corners**, sew 1 to each end of Top and Bottom Outer Borders. Sew Top and Bottom Outer Borders to quilt top. Again, it may be necessary to make border seams wider or narrower to adjust the length to fit the quilt top.

Star Block Diagram
(make 3)

Additional Star Block Diagrams
(make 3 of each color way)

Row 1
(make 4)

Row 2
(make 3)

Border Corner (make 4)

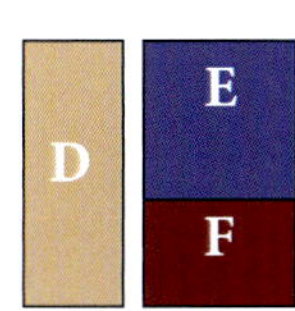

Quilt Top Diagram

FINISHING THE QUILT

1. Stay-stitch around the outside edge of the quilt top to keep seams from opening during quilting.

2. Follow **Quilting,** page 63, to mark, layer, and quilt. Our quilt is machine quilted with an all-over meandering pattern on the quilt top center, a straight line through the center of the inner border, and wavy lines in each rectangle of the outer border.

3. Sew **binding strips** together using a diagonal seam (Fig. 4) to make a continuous binding strip.
4. Follow **Attaching Binding with Mitered Corners,** page 66, and attach binding.

Fig. 4

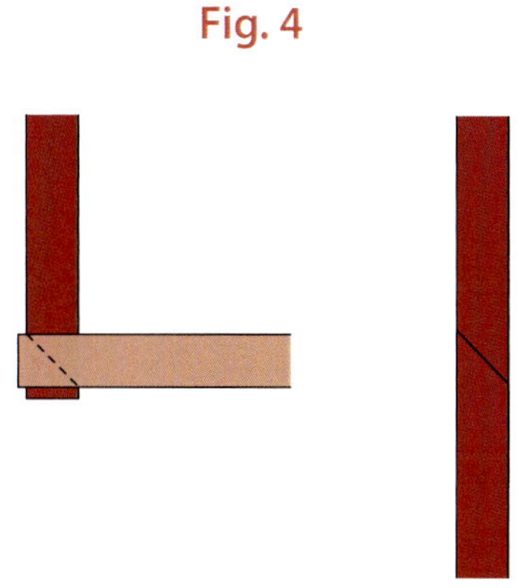

¼ Diamond Block (make 68 photocopies)

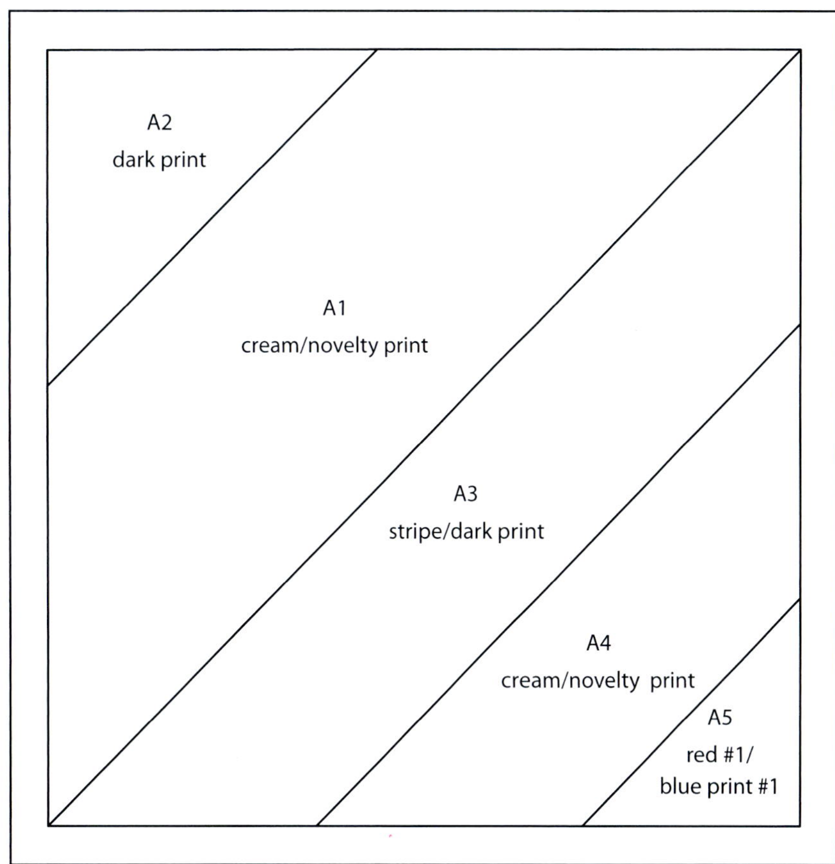

Pinwheel Tapestry

Finished Quilt Size: 87" x 96" (221 cm x 244 cm)
Finished Block Size: 9" x 9" (23 cm x 23 cm)

SHOPPING LIST

Yardage is based on 43"/44" (109 cm/112 cm) wide fabric with a usable widthof 40" (102 cm). Fat quarters are approximately 22" x 18" (56 cm x 46 cm).

- ☐ 27 fat quarters of assorted tan, brown, red, and black prints for blocks and Flying Geese border
- ☐ 14 fat quarters of assorted light prints for block backgrounds and Flying Geese border
- ☐ 1 yd (91 cm) of black solid fabric for narrow borders
- ☐ 2½ yds (2.3 m) of red paisley print fabric for outer border and blocks
- ☐ 8 yds (7.3 m) of fabric for backing
- ☐ 1 yd (91 cm) of brown print fabric for binding
- ☐ 95" x 104" (241 cm x 264 cm) piece of batting

CUTTING THE PIECES

Note: To achieve the scrappy look of our quilt, you may want to mix and match the print fabrics and background fabrics. We also used some of the red paisley border fabric in our blocks. Cut your borders and binding first to ensure that you have enough fabric.

*Follow **Rotary Cutting,** page 55, to cut fabric. Cut all strips from the selvage-to-selvage width of the fabric. Cut strips from fat quarters parallel to the long edge. Borders are cut exact length. All measurements include ¼" seam allowances.*

From assorted dark print fat quarters:

- Cut 56 matching sets of 4 **rectangles A** 7" x 3".
- Cut 56 squares C 4½" x 4½".

From assorted light print fat quarters:

- Cut 56 matching sets of 8 **squares B** 3" x 3".

From black solid fabric:

- Cut 16 strips 2" wide.

From red paisley print fabric:

- Cut 2 lengthwise **side outer borders** 6" x 84½".
- Cut 2 lengthwise **top/bottom outer borders** 6" x 87½".

From brown print fabric for binding:

- Cut 10 **binding strips** 2½" wide.

MAKING THE BLOCKS

*Follow **Piecing,** page 56, and **Pressing,** page 57, to make the quilt top. Use ¼" seam allowances throughout. As you stitch the units for the **Pinwheel Blocks,** you will also be sewing "bonus" Triangle-Squares which will be used to make the pieced border. Set these aside to use in border construction.*

1. For each block, you will need:
   - 4 matching medium/dark print **rectangles A.**
   - 8 matching light print **squares B.**
   - 1 medium/dark print **square C.**

2. Draw a diagonal line on the wrong side of each **square B.**

3. Matching right sides, place 1 **square B** on the left edge of 1 **rectangle A.** Stitch on the drawn line. Then stitch a scant ½" from the drawn line ***(Fig. 1)***.

Fig. 1

4. Cut between the stitched lines ***(Fig. 2)*** to make 1 **Triangle-Square** and 1 **Unit 1.** Press the seam allowances toward the darker fabric. Make 4 **Unit 1's** and 4 **Triangle-Squares.** Set aside the **Triangle-Squares** for the **Flying Geese Border.**

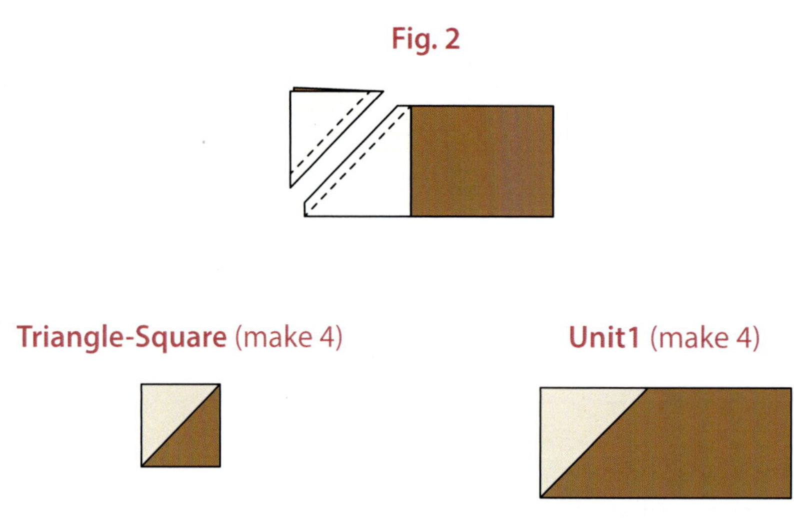

5. In the same manner, stitch a light print **square B** to the right edge of **Unit 1** ***(Fig. 3)*** to make **Unit 2** and a **Triangle-Square.** Make 4 **Unit 2's** and 4 **Triangle-Squares.** Set aside the **Triangle-Squares** for the **Flying Geese Border.**

6. Referring to the **Assembly Diagram**, arrange 4 matching **Unit 2's** and 1 contrasting **square C**. The first seam will be a partial seam because you will only sew it part of the way. Sew a **square C** to a **Unit 2** , stopping about 1½"-2" from the end of the seam ***(Fig. 4)***. Finger-press the seam allowances toward the **square C**. Working counter clockwise, sew the remaining 3 **Unit 2's** to **square C**. When you have sewn on the last unit, finish the partial seam to complete the **Pinwheel Block**.

Fig. 4

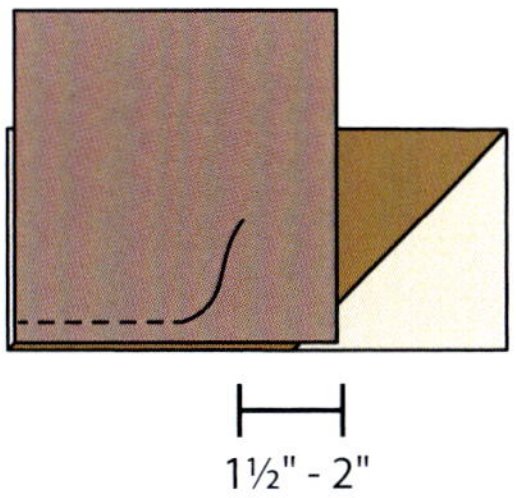

Assembly Diagram

Pinwheel Block

7. Repeat Steps 1-6 to make a total of 56 Blocks.

ASSEMBLING THE QUILT TOP

*Refer to **Quilt Top Diagram** to assemble the quilt top.*

1. Arrange and then sew the Blocks into 8 rows of 7 blocks each to make the **quilt top center.**

2. For the **inner narrow border,** sew the solid black strips together end-to-end to make one continuous **narrow border strip.** Cut 2 side **inner narrow borders** 72½" long and **2 top/bottom inner narrow borders** 66½" long from the narrow border strip. Matching centers and corner, sew the side then **top/bottom inner narrow borders** to the **quilt top center.**

3. For the **Flying Geese Border,** trim 392 **Triangle-Squares** to 2" x 2". Sew 2 **Triangle-Squares** together to make a **Flying Geese Unit.**
   Make a total of 196 **Flying Geese Units.**

Flying Geese Unit
(make 196)

4. Sew 50 **Flying Geese Units** together to make a **Flying Geese Side Border.** Make 2 **Flying Geese Side Borders.** Referring to the photo for the correct orientation, sew 1 **Flying Geese Side Border** to each side of the quilt. Press the seam allowances toward the first inner borders.

5. Sew 44 **Flying Geese** together to make the **Flying Geese Top Border.** Repeat for the **Flying Geese Bottom Border.**

6. Sew together 2 **Flying Geese Units** to make a **Double Geese Block.** Make a total of 4 **Double Geese Blocks.**

Double Geese Block
(make 4)

7. Sew a **Double Geese Block** to each end of the **Flying Geese** top and bottom borders. Referring to the photo for the correct orientation of the borders, stitch the borders to the quilt. Press the seam allowances toward the solid black borders.

8. Cut 2 **side outer narrow borders** 81½" long and 2 **top/bottom outer narrow borders** 75½" long from the narrow border strip. Matching centers and corner, sew the side then top/bottom outer narrow borders to the quilt top center.

9. Matching centers and corner, sew the side then **top/bottom outer borders** to the quilt top center.

COMPLETING THE QUILT

1. Follow **Quilting,** page 63, to mark, layer, and quilt as desired. Quilt shown has meandering quilting in the light color block backgrounds. The dark pinwheels and the Flying Geese Border are outline quilted with curved lines. The narrow borders have a wavy feather design and the outer border has channel quilting spaced about 1½" apart.

2. Follow **Making a Hanging Sleeve,** page 65, if a hanging sleeve is desired.

3. Use **binding strips** and follow **Binding,** page 65, to bind quilt.

Quilt Top Diagram

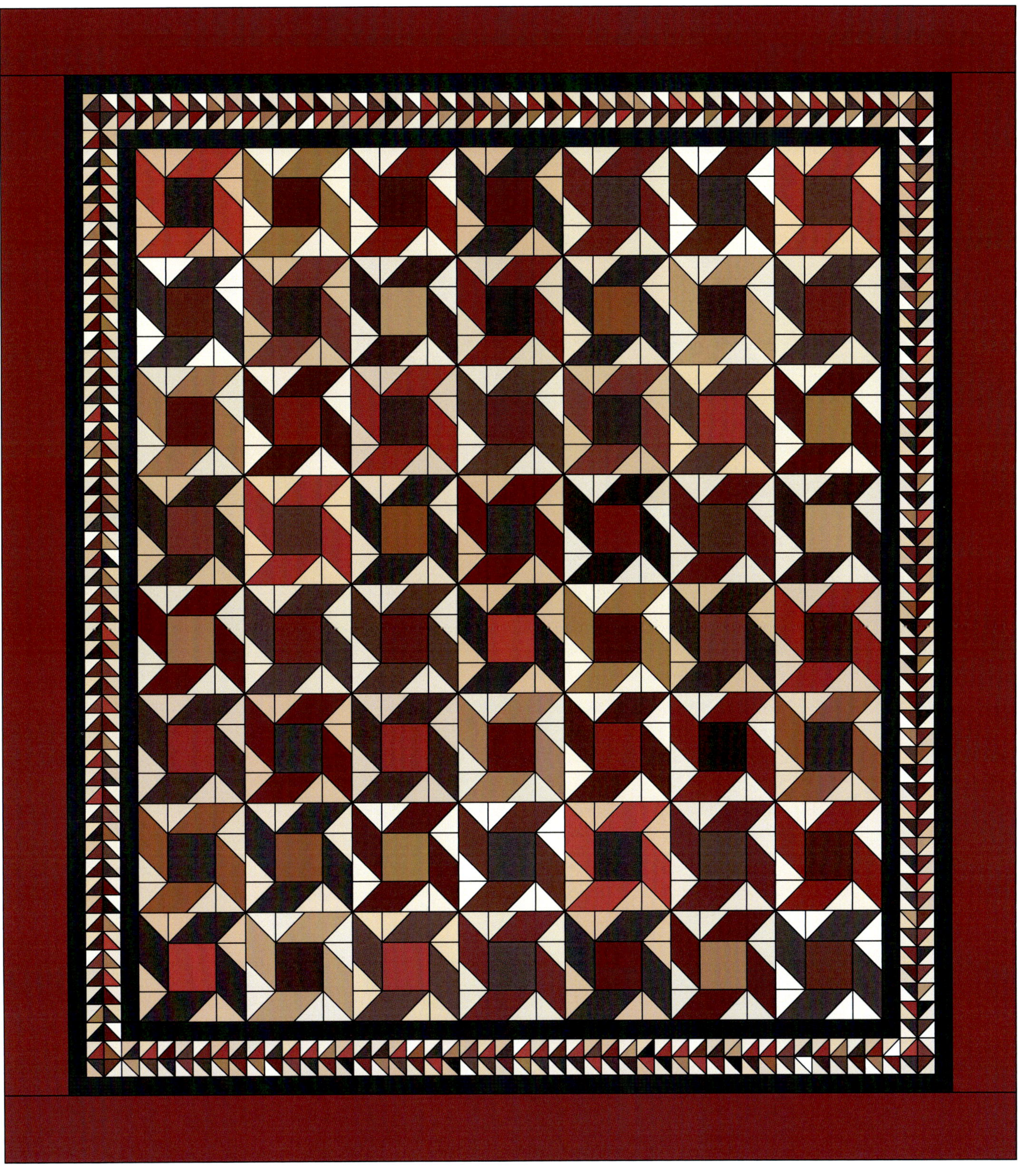

Kriss-Cross

Finished Quilt Size: 62" x 71" (157 cm x 180 cm)
Finished Block Size: 9" x 9" (23 cm x 23 cm)

To create the scrappy look of this quilt, mix and match the various fabrics in each block. The cutting instructions provide you with a few extra squares and strips to allow you the freedom to play with block design. To increase the scrappy look, add a few additional fat eighths or scraps from your stash.

SHOPPING LIST

Yardage is based on 43"/44" (109 cm/112 cm) wide fabric with a usable width of 40" (102 cm). A fat quarter measures approximately 22" x 18" (56 cm x 46 cm.)

- ☐ 15-16 fat quarters or approximately 4 yds (3.7 m) **total** of coordinating print fabrics for blocks
- ☐ ⅞ yd (80 cm) of red print fabric for inner border and bindings
- ☐ 2 yds (1.8 m) of floral print fabric for outer border
- ☐ 4½ yds (4.1 m) of fabric for backing
- ☐ 70" x 79" (178 cm x 201 cm) piece of batting

CUTTING THE PIECES

Follow ***Rotary Cutting****, page 55, to cut fabric. For yardage, cut all strips from the selvage-to-selvage width of the fabric unless otherwise stated. For fat quarters, cut strips parallel to the short edge. Outer borders are cut longer than needed and will be trimmed to fit quilt top center. All measurements include ¼" seam allowances.*

From each fat quarter:

- Cut 6 **short strips** 1½" x 18".
- Cut 2 strips 3½" x 18". From these strips, cut 10 **squares** 3½" x 3½".

From red print fabric:

- Cut 6 **inner border strips** 1½" wide.
- Cut 8 **binding strips** 2¼" wide.

From floral print fabric:

- Cut 2 *lengthwise* **outer side borders** 7½" x 60½".
- Cut 2 *lengthwise* **outer top/bottom borders** 7½" x 65½".

MAKING THE BLOCKS

*Follow **Machine Piecing,** page 56, and **Pressing,** page 57, to make quilt top. Use ¼" seam allowances throughout.*

1. Sew together 2 matching **short strips** and one contrasting **short strip**. Press the seam allowances toward the center strip. Cut the pieced strip into four 3½" segments ***(Fig. 1)***.

Fig. 1

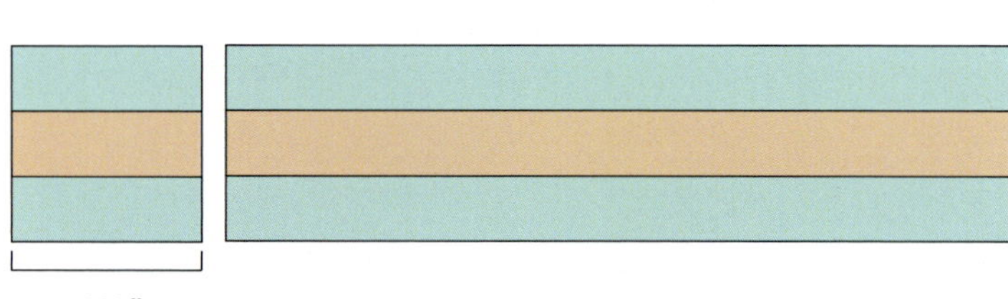

2. Arrange 4 matching **squares**, 1 contrasting **square**, and 4 pieced segments. Sew the pieces together in rows, pressing the seam allowances away from the pieced segments. Sew the rows together. Repeat to make a **total** of 30 Blocks.

Block (make 30)

ASSEMBLING THE QUILT TOP

*Refer to **Quilt Top** to assemble quilt top.*

1. Sew 5 Blocks together to make a Row. Make 6 Rows. Sew the Rows together.

2. Using diagonal seams, sew **inner border strips** together to make one continuous strip ***(Fig. 2)***.

Fig. 2

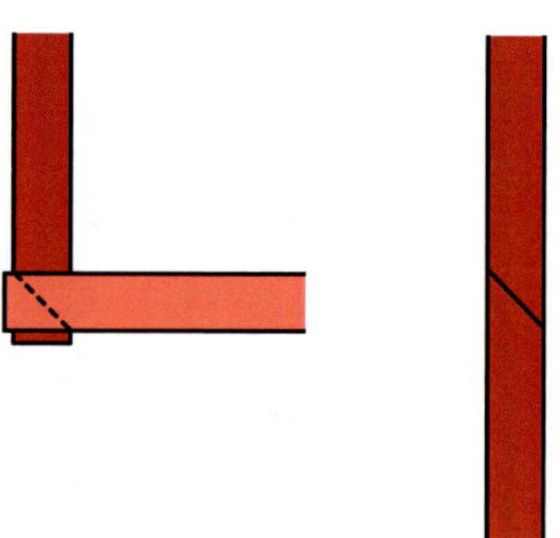

3. Measure *length* across center of quilt top center. Cut 2 **inner side borders** from continuous strip. Matching centers and corners, sew inner side borders to quilt top center.

4. Measure *width* across center of quilt top center (including added borders). Cut 2 **inner top/bottom borders** from continuous strip. Matching centers and corners, sew inner top/bottom borders to quilt top center.

5. Repeat Steps 3-4 to add **outer side**, then **outer top/bottom borders**.

Quilt Top

COMPLETING THE QUILT

1. Follow **Quilting,** page 63, to mark, layer, and quilt as desired. Quilt shown is quilted with an all-over leaf design in the quilt top center, in the ditch along each border, and a feather design in the outer border.

2. Follow **Making a Hanging Sleeve,** page 65, if a hanging sleeve is desired.

3. Sew **binding strips** together end to end diagonally. Follow **Attaching Binding with Mitered Corners,** page 66, to bind quilt.

Homeward Bound

Finished Quilt Size: 82½" x 97⅞" (221 cm x 244 cm)
Finished Block Size: 9" x 9" (23 cm x 23 cm)

SHOPPING LIST

Yardage is based on 43"/44" (109 cm/112 cm) wide fabric with a usable width of 40" (102 cm).

- ☐ 2½ yds (2.3 m) of tan/red small floral print fabric for setting triangles and inner border
- ☐ 2½ yds (2.3 m) of brown print fabric for outer border and binding
- ☐ ¾ yd (69 cm) of dark blue print fabric for vine
- ☐ 2⅛ yds (1.9 m) **total** of assorted light/medium print fabrics for blocks
- ☐ 5½ yds (3.3 m) **total** of assorted dark print fabrics for blocks and leaves
- ☐ 7⅝ yds (7 m) of fabric for backing

You will also need:

- ☐ 90½" x 99" (230 cm x 251 cm) piece of batting Template plastic
- ☐ Optional: ½" (13 mm) bias pressing bar

CUTTING THE PIECES

*Follow **Rotary Cutting,** page 55, to cut fabric. Borders include extra length for "insurance" and will be trimmed after assembling quilt top center. The side setting triangles and corner setting triangles are over-cut and will be trimmed after assembly. All measurements include ¼" seam allowances. Use pattern, page 27, and follow **Making and Using Templates,** page 58, to make appliqué template for the leaf.*

From tan/red small floral print fabric:

- Cut 2 *lengthwise* side inner borders 6½" x 72⅜".
- Cut 2 *lengthwise* top/bottom inner borders 6½" x 76".

From the remaining width:

- Cut 3 strips 10"w. From these strips, cut 7 squares 10" x 10". Cut each square ***twice*** diagonally to make 28 side setting triangles. You will use 26 triangles and have 2 left over.
- Cut 2 squares 5⅜" x 5⅜". Cut each square ***once*** diagonally to make 4 corner setting triangles.

From brown print fabric:

- Cut 2 *lengthwise* side outer borders 5½" x 84⅜".
- Cut 2 *lengthwise* top/bottom outer borders 5½" x 86".
- Cut 5 *lengthwise* binding strips 2½" x 90".

From dark blue print fabric:

- Cut 1 square 24" x 24". Refer to **Making a Continuous Bias Strip,** page 65, to cut 1 bias strip for vine 1½" x 300".

From assorted light/medium print fabrics (including remaining tan/red small floral print fabrics):

- Cut 49 matching sets of 3 squares 3" x 3" and 3 squares 2⅞" x 2⅞". Cut the 2⅞" x 2⅞" squares ***once*** diagonally to make 6 small triangles.

From assorted dark print fabrics (including remaining brown print and dark blue print fabrics:

- Cut 49 matching sets of 1 square 6⅞" x 6⅞" and 3 squares 3" x 3". Cut the larger square ***once*** diagonally to make 2 large triangles.
- Use template to cut 132 leaves.

ASSEMBLING THE BLOCKS

*Follow **Machine Piecing,** page 56, and **Pressing,** page 57, and use a ¼" seam allowance.*

1. Draw a diagonal line on wrong side of each assorted light/medium print square. With right sides together, place 1 light/medium print square on top of 1 dark print square. Stitch ¼" from each side of drawn line ***(Fig. 1)***.

Fig. 1

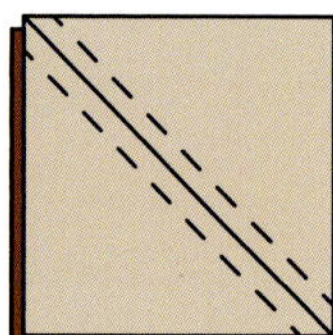

2. Cut along drawn line and press open, pressing seam allowances toward darker fabric to make 2 **Triangle-Squares**. Make 49 sets of 6 matching **Triangle-Squares**. Trim each **Triangle-Square** to 2½" x 2½".

Triangle-Squares
(make 49 sets of 6)

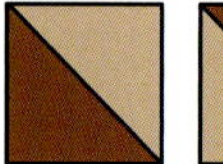
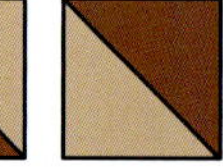

3. Refer to **Fig. 2** to sew 3 matching light/medium triangles and 3 **Triangles-Squares** together to make **Unit 1**. Make 49 sets of 2 matching **Unit 1's**.

Fig. 2

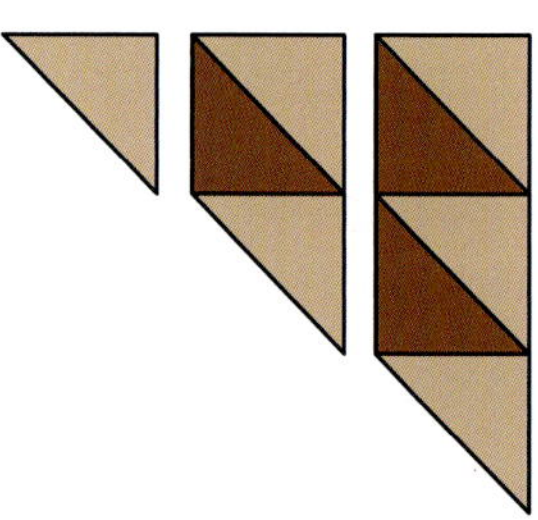

Unit 1
(make 49 sets of 2)

4. Sew matching large triangle to **Unit 1** to make **Block**. Make 49 sets of 2 matching **Blocks**.

Block
(make 49 sets of 2)

ASSEMBLING THE QUILT TOP

Refer to ***Assembly Diagram****, page 29.*

1. Sew side setting triangles and Blocks together in diagonal rows. Sew rows together. Sew corner setting triangles to corners. Trim quilt top edges ¼" from corners of blocks.

2. Refer to **Adding Squared Borders,** page 62, to add side, then top and bottom inner borders to quilt top.

3. In same manner, sew side, then top and bottom outer borders to quilt top.

ADDING THE APPLIQUÉS

1. Matching wrong sides, fold bias strip for vine in half. Stitch ¼" from raw edge. Trim seam allowances to ⅛" ***(Fig. 3)***. Press vine flat, centering seam allowances on back so raw edge isn't visible from front. Using a ½" bias pressing bar makes pressing faster and easier.

Fig. 3

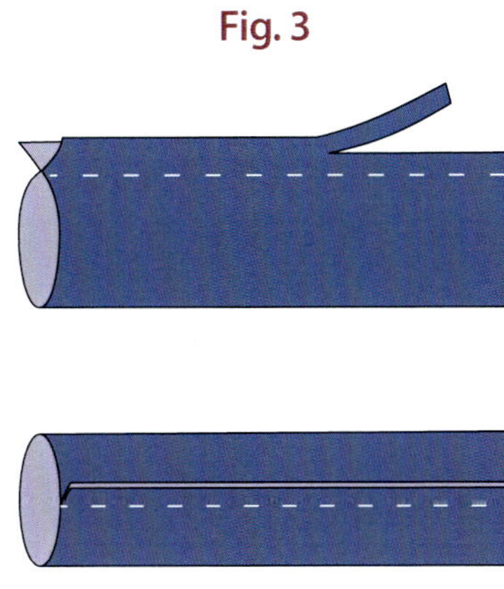

2. Pin vine to inner border, trimming and tucking ends under as needed.

3. Refer to **Blind Stitch,** page 68, to stitch vine in place.

4. Pin leaves to inner border. Refer to **Needle-Turn Appliqué,** page 58, to stitch leaves in place.

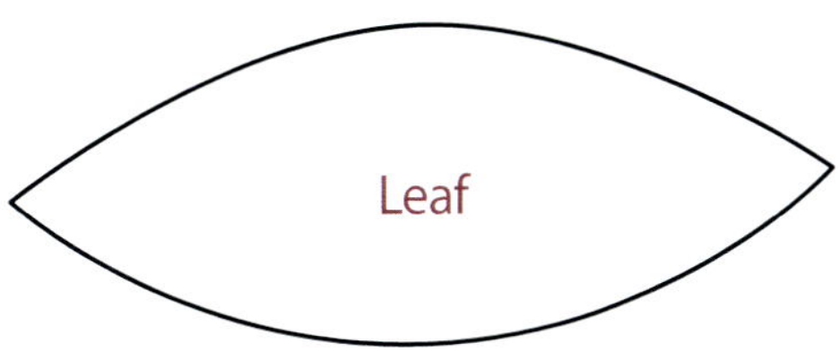

COMPLETING THE QUILT

1. Follow **Quilting,** page 63, to mark, layer, and quilt as desired. Quilt shown is machine quilted with an all-over feather design in the blocks. The vine and leaves are echo quilted. The outer border is filled with channel quilting ¾" apart, perpendicular to the border seams.

2. Sew **binding strips** together using a diagonal seam ***(Fig. 4)*** to make a **continuous binding strip.**

3. Follow **Attaching Binding With Mitered Corners,** page 66, to attach binding.

Fig. 4

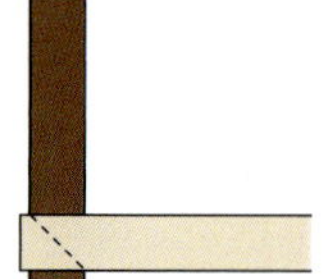

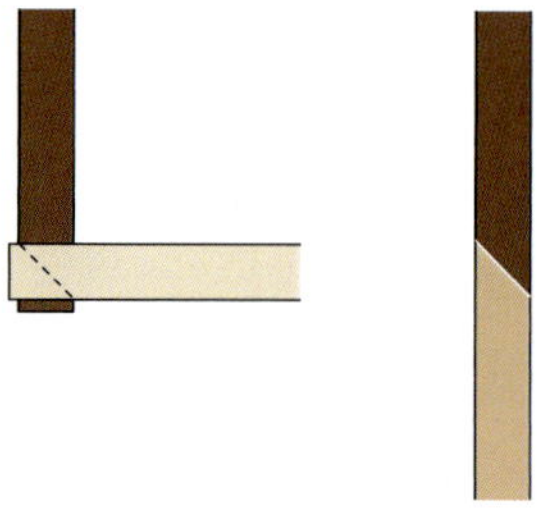

Assembly Diagram

It's Twirl Time

Finished Quilt Size: 44" x 54" (112 cm x 137 cm)
Finished Block Size: 10" x 10" (25 cm x 25 cm)

SHOPPING LIST

Yardage is based on 43"/44" (109 cm/112 cm) wide fabric with a usable width of 40" (102 cm). Fat quarters are approximately 22" x 18" (56 cm x 46 cm).

- ☐ 1¼ yds (1.1 m) **total *or*** 5-6 fat quarters of assorted light print fabrics for block backgrounds and inner border
- ☐ 1½ yds (1.4 m) **total *or*** 6 fat quarters of assorted dark print fabrics for blocks and outer borders
- ☐ ⅜ yd (34 cm) of medium print fabric for block centers
- ☐ 2¼ yds (2.1 m) of fabric for backing
- ☐ ½ yd (57 cm) of fabric for binding
- ☐ 52" x 62" (132 cm x 157 cm) piece of batting

CUTTING THE PIECES

*Follow **Rotary Cutting,** page 55, to cut fabric. Cut all strips from the selvage-to-selvage width of the fabric. Cut strips from fat quarters parallel to the long edge. All measurements include ¼" seam allowances.*

From assorted light print fabrics:

- Cut a **total** of 170 **squares B** 2½" x 2½".
- Cut a **total** of 48 **rectangles** C 2½" x 4½".

From assorted dark print fabrics:

- Cut a **total** of 48 **squares A** 4½" x 4½".
- Cut 2 **border rectangles** 5½" x 14½".
- Cut 4 **border rectangles** 5½" x 12½".
- Cut 6 **border rectangles** 5½" x 9½".
- Cut 7 **border rectangles** 5½" x 7½".
- Cut 3 **border squares** 5½" x 5½".

From medium print fabric:

- Cut 60 **squares B** 2½" x 2½".

From binding fabric:

- Cut 6 **binding strips** 2¼" wide.

MAKING THE BLOCKS

*Follow **Piecing,** page 56, and **Pressing,** page 57, to make the quilt top. Use ¼" seam allowances throughout.*

1. To make 2 **Blocks**, you will need:
   - 16 light print **squares B**
   - 8 light print **rectangles C**
   - 8 dark print **squares A**
   - 10 medium print **squares B**

2. Draw a diagonal line on the wrong side of 16 matching light print **squares B**. Place a **square B** on the corner of a dark print **square A**. Stitch on the drawn line ***(Fig. 1)***. trim seam allowance to ¼" ***(Fig. 2)*** and press open ***(Fig. 3)***.

Fig. 1

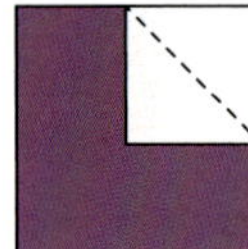

Fig. 2

Fig. 3

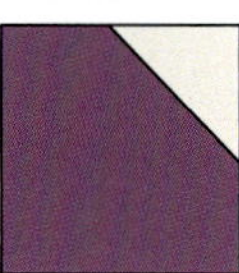

3. In the same manner, sew a light print **square B** to the opposite corner of the dark print **square A *(Fig. 4)***.

Fig. 4

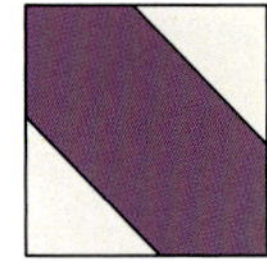

4. Sew a medium print **square B** to a remaining corner of dark print **square A** to make **Unit 1**. Make 8 **Unit 1's**.

Unit 1 (make 8)

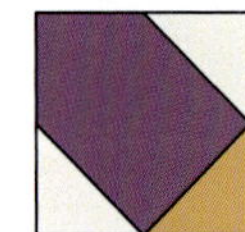

5. Sew a matching light print **rectangle C** to the left side of each **Unit 1** to make **Unit 2**. Make 8 **Unit 2's**.

Unit 2 (make 8)

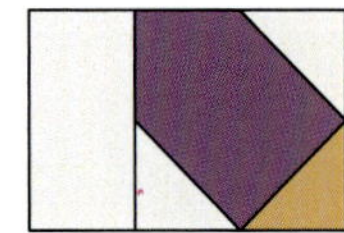

6. Arrange 4 **Unit 2's** and 1 medium **square B** as shown in **Block Diagram**. The **Unit 1** positioned above the **square B** will be sewn to the **square B** with a partial seam ***(Fig. 5)***, indicated by the red dot. Once you have sewn the partial seam, continue adding **Unit 1's** clockwise ***(Fig. 6)***. Complete the partial seam to finish the block. Make 2 matching blocks.

Fig. 5

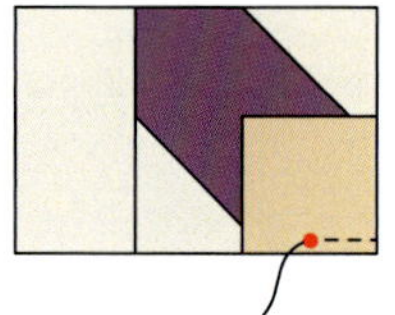

Fig. 6

Block Diagram
(make 2)

7. Repeat Steps 2-6 to make a total of 6 pairs of blocks (12 blocks total).

ASSEMBLING THE QUILT TOP

*Refer to **Quilt Top Diagram** to assemble the quilt top.*

1. To make quilt top center, arrange the **Blocks** in 4 rows of 3 blocks each. Sew the rows together.

2. To make 1 **inner side border**, sew together 20 light **squares B**, pressing seam allowances in 1 direction. Repeat to make a total of 2 **inner side borders**.

3. Sew 1 inner side border to each side of quilt top center.

4. To make 1 **inner top/bottom border**, sew together 17 light **squares B**, pressing seam allowances in 1 direction. Repeat to make a total of 2 **inner top/bottom borders.**

5. Sew **inner top/bottom borders** to quilt top center.

6. For the **outer borders**, sew assorted dark print **border rectangles** and **squares** together end to end. From this piece, cut 4 **outer borders** 44½" long.

7. Sew 1 **outer border** to each side of the quilt top; press seam allowances toward the borders. Sew top and bottom outer border to the quilt top; press seam allowances toward the borders.

Quilt Top Diagram

COMPLETING THE QUILT

1. Follow **Quilting,** page 63, to mark, layer, and quilt as desired. Quilt shown is quilted with a large leaf and vine pattern in the outer border and a zigzag in the inner border. The blocks have swirls in the center star, large leaves in the petals, and a small leaf and vine in the background.

2. Follow **Making a Hanging Sleeve,** page 65, if a hanging sleeve is desired.

3. Use **binding strips** and follow **Binding,** page 66, to bind quilt.

Save Your Scraps

Finished Quilt Size: 64" x 64" (221 cm x 244 cm)
Finished Block Size: 9" x 9" (23 cm x 23 cm)

SHOPPING LIST

Yardage is based on 43"/44" (109 cm/112 cm) wide fabric with a usable width of 40" (102 cm). A fat quarter measures approximately 22" x 18" (56 cm x 46 cm).

- ☐ 1½ - 2 yds (1.4 m - 1.8 m) **total** of assorted light print fabrics for Double Nine Patch and Shoo Fly Blocks
- ☐ 2 - 2¼ yds (1.8 m - 2.1 m) **total** of assorted medium and dark print fabrics for blocks and binding
- ☐ ⅜ yd (34 cm) **total** of assorted blue print fabrics for Shoo Fly Blocks
- ☐ ⅝ yd (57 cm) **total** of assorted rust print fabrics for inner border and Prairie Dresden Block centers
- ☐ 1 yd (91 cm) of light tone-on-tone print fabric for Prairie Dresden Block backgrounds
- ☐ 1⅞ yds (1.7 m) of blue print fabric for outer border
- ☐ 4 yds (3.7 m) of fabric for backing
- ☐ 72" x 72" (183 cm x 183 cm) piece of batting
- ☐ EZ Quilting® Easy Dresden Quilt Ruler
- ☐ Pieces Be With You® Prairie Pointer Pressing Tool
- ☐ freezer paper
- ☐ liquid starch
- ☐ small paintbrush
- ☐ chopstick or awl
- ☐ fabric glue (optional)

CUTTING THE PIECES

Follow ***Rotary Cutting****, page 55, to cut fabric. For yardage, cut all strips from the selvage-to-selvage width of the fabric unless otherwise stated. For fat quarters, cut strips parallel to the long edge. Outer border strips are cut longer than needed and will be trimmed to fit quilt top center. All measurements include ¼" seam allowances.*

From assorted light print fabrics:

- Cut 240 **squares A** 1½" x 1½".
- Cut 80 **squares B** 3½" x 3½".

From assorted medium and dark print fabrics:

- Cut 2½" wide **strips** to total approximately 280" of length for the Dresden Wedges.
- Cut 300 **squares A** 1½" x 1½".
- Cut assorted **binding strips** 2¼" wide in various lengths to total 8 yds when sewn together diagonally end to end.

From assorted blue print fabrics:

- Cut 16 **squares A** 1½" x 1½".
- Cut 4 **squares B** 3½" x 3½".

From assorted rust print fabrics:

- Cut assorted **inner border strips** 2½" wide in random lengths to total approximately 220" when sewn together diagonally end to end.

From light tone-on-tone print fabric:

- Cut 9 **background squares** 10" x 10".

From blue print fabric:

- Cut 2 *lengthwise* **outer side borders** 7½" x 49½".
- Cut 2 *lengthwise* **outer top/bottom borders** 7½" x 67½".

MAKING THE PRAIRIE DRESDEN BLOCKS

*Follow **Machine Piecing**, page 56, and **Pressing**, page 57, to make quilt top. Use ¼" seam allowances throughout.*

1. For the **Dresden Wedges**, align the 2½" line on the Easy Dresden Ruler with the top edge of a strip. Cut along each side of the ruler to cut a wedge. Rotate the ruler and align the 2½" line on the ruler with the bottom edge of the strip; cut. Repeat this process ***(Fig. 1)*** until you have cut a total of 180 wedges.

Fig. 1

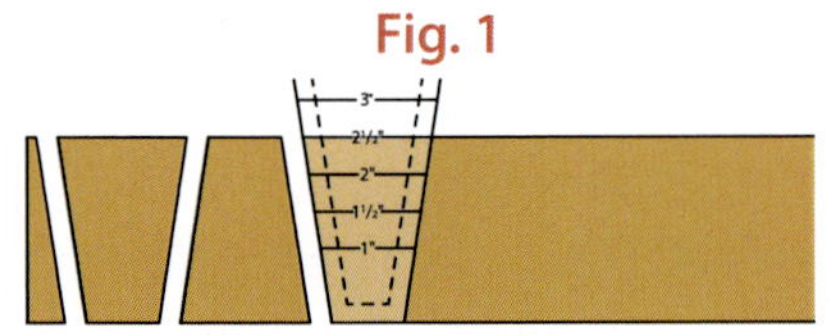

2. For each wedge, fold the wide end, right sides together, and stitch using a short stitch length ***(Fig. 2)***. Trim the point from the folded edge at an angle ***(Fig. 3)***. Using the Prairie Pointer Pressing Tool, align the seam with the center line on the tool; press the seam open ***(Fig. 4)***. Turn wedge right side out; insert pressing tool and press ***(Fig. 5)***.

Fig. 2 **Fig. 3**

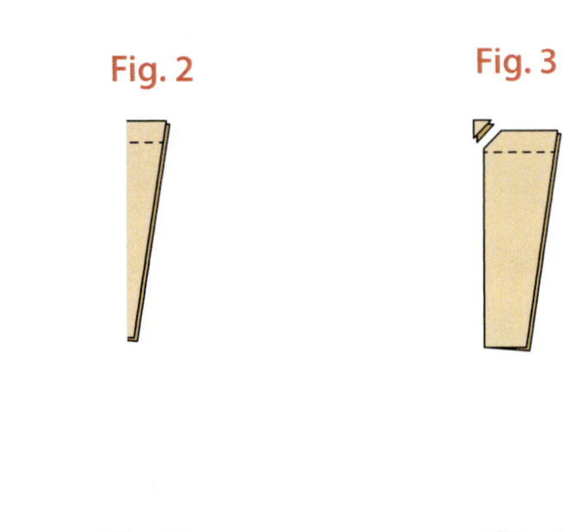

Fig. 4 **Fig. 5**

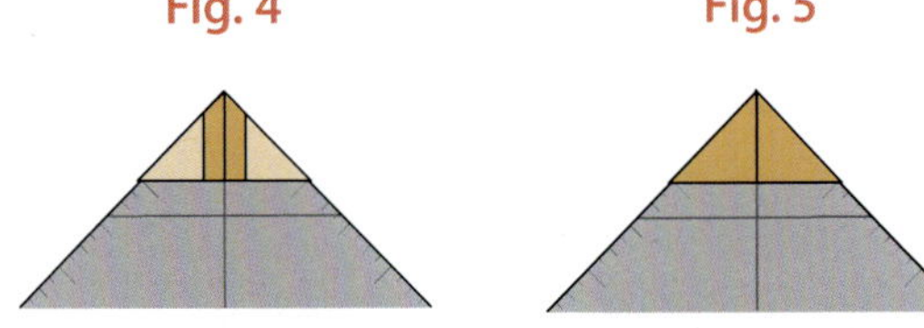

3. Matching **right** sides and aligning the pointed ends, place 2 wedges together. Backstitching at beginning and end and beginning stitching at the folded edge, sew the wedges together along one edge ***(Fig. 6)***; press open. Join five wedges in this manner. Press seam allowances open. Make a total of 36 **Wedge Units**.

Fig. 6

Wedge Unit (make 36)

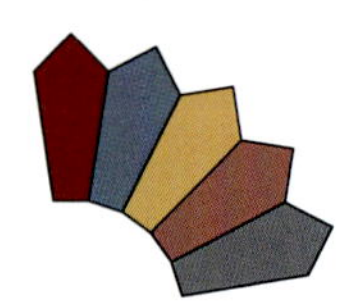

4. Sew 4 Wedge Units together to make a **Dresden Flower**. Make a total of 9 **Dresden Flowers**.

Dresden Flower (make 9)

5. Press each **background square** horizontally and vertically through the center to create registration marks.

6. Aligning the points of the wedges with the registration marks, position a **Dresden Flower** on a **background square**; pin or glue the flower in place with small dabs of glue.

7. Trace the circle template 9 times onto freezer paper. Keeping both pieces dull side up, press the traced freezer paper to an unmarked sheet of freezer paper. Cut out the two-layered freezer paper templates.

8. Position one template on the wrong side of the rust print fabric. Iron the template to the fabric, shiny side down. Trim fabric, leaving an approximately ⅜" seam allowance.

9. Use the paintbrush to brush starch on the seam allowance. Incrementally turn the seam allowance over the edge of the freezer paper circle using a chopstick or awl, adding starch and pressing the seam allowance in place as you go. Remove the freezer paper.

Circle Template

10. Position the circle on the flower. Pin or glue the circle in place with small dabs of glue. Refer to **Blind Stitch,** page 68, to sew the circle in place.

11. Press the block from the **wrong** side. Centering the flower, trim the block to 9½" x 9½" to make the **Prairie Dresden Block**. Make a total of 9 **Prairie Dresden Blocks**.

Prairie Dresden Block

MAKING THE DOUBLE NINE PATCH BLOCKS

1. Sew together four light print **squares A** and five medium or dark print **squares A** to make a **Nine Patch Block**. Sew the squares together in rows, pressing the seam allowances toward the darker fabric. Sew the rows together. Make 60 **Nine Patch Blocks**.

Nine Patch Block (make 60)

2. Sew together four light print **squares B** and five **Nine Patch Blocks** to make a **Double Nine Patch Block**. Sew the units together in rows, pressing the seam allowances toward the **squares B**. Sew the rows together. Make 12 **Double Nine Patch Blocks**.

Double Nine Patch Block (make 12)

MAKING THE SHOO FLY BLOCKS

1. Draw a diagonal line from corner to corner on the wrong side of the blue print **squares A**. Matching right sides, place one blue print **square A** on one light print **square B**. Stitch on the drawn line; trim the seam allowances to ¼" ***(Fig. 7)***. Press the triangle to the right side to make **Unit 1**. Make 16 **Unit 1's**.

Unit 1 (make 16)

Fig. 7

2. Sew together four light print **squares B**, one blue print **square B**, and four **Unit 1's** to make a **Shoo Fly Block**. Sew the pieces together in rows, pressing the seam allowances toward the **squares B**. Sew the rows together. Make 4 **Shoo Fly Blocks**.

Shoo Fly Block (make 4)

ASSEMBLING THE QUILT TOP

*Refer to **Quilt Top Diagram** to assemble quilt top.*

1. Sew the blocks together in rows. Sew the rows together.

2. Using diagonal seams, sew **inner border strips** together to make one continuous strip ***(Fig. 8)***.

Fig. 8

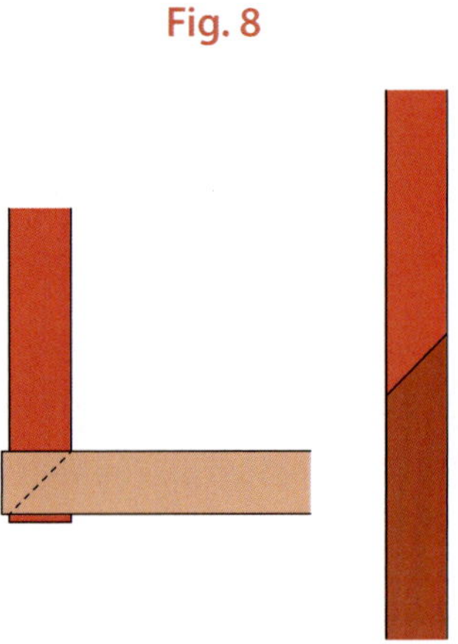

3. Measure *length* across center of quilt top center. Cut 2 **inner side borders** from continuous strip. Matching centers and corners, sew inner side borders to quilt top center.

4. Measure *width* across center of quilt top center (including added borders). Cut 2 **inner top/bottom borders** from continuous strip. Matching centers and corners, sew inner top/bottom borders to quilt top center.

5. Repeat Steps 3-4 to add **outer side**, then **outer top/bottom borders**.

Quilt Top Diagram

COMPLETING THE QUILT

1. Follow **Quilting,** page 63, to mark, layer, and quilt as desired. Quilt shown is quilted with feathers around the Prairie Dresden Blocks and along the outer borders and with an all-over leaf design over the remainder of the quilt.

2. Follow **Making a Hanging Sleeve,** page 65, if a hanging sleeve is desired.

3. Sew binding strips together end to end diagonally. Follow **Attaching Binding with Mitered Corners,** page 66, to bind quilt.

Trafalgar Square

Finished Quilt Size: 65" x 73" (165 cm x 185 cm)
Finished Block Size: 8" x 8" (20 cm x 20 cm)

SHOPPING LIST

Yardage is based on 43"/44" (109 cm/112 cm) wide fabric with a usable width of 40" (102 cm). A fat quarter measures approximately 22" x 18" (53 cm x 46 cm).

- ☐ fat quarter each of four assorted red prints for Night Crossing Blocks, flowers, and circle flower centers
- ☐ fat quarter each of two assorted black prints for Night Crossing Blocks
- ☐ fat quarter of black medium scale floral print fabric for Framed Square Block centers and flower centers
- ☐ fat quarter of black and red floral print fabric for Framed Square Block centers and Night Crossing Blocks
- ☐ fat quarter of black, red, and white print fabric for Framed Square Block centers and Night Crossing Blocks
- ☐ ½ yd (46 cm) of ivory and black print fabric for Night Crossing Block centers and leaves
- ☐ ⅜ yd (34 cm) of ivory print fabric for Night Crossing Blocks
- ☐ ½ yd (46 cm) of red and black stripe fabric for blocks
- ☐ ½ yd (46 cm) of black and red stripe fabric for Framed Square Blocks
- ☐ ½ yd (46 cm) of ivory and red print fabric for borders #1 and circle flowers
- ☐ 1¼ yds (1.1 m) of black and ivory trailing floral print fabric for borders #2 and Night Crossing Blocks
- ☐ ⅝ yd (57 cm) of floral trellis print fabric for borders #3 and Framed Square Block centers
- ☐ 1⅜ yds (1.3 m) of black, red, and tan small print fabric for borders #4
- ☐ ¾ yd (69 cm) of black and ivory stripe fabric for Night Crossing Blocks and binding
- ☐ 4½ yds (4.1 m) of fabric for backing
- ☐ 1½ yds (1.4 m) of 17" (43 cm) wide paper-backed fusible web
- ☐ 73" x 81" (185 cm x 206 cm) piece of batting
- ☐ stabilizer

CUTTING THE PIECES

Follow **Rotary Cutting,** *page 55, to cut fabric. For yardage, cut all strips from the selvage-to-selvage width of the fabric unless otherwise stated. For fat quarters, cut strips parallel to the short edge. Mitered borders are cut longer than needed and will be trimmed to fit quilt top center. All measurements include ¼" seam allowances.*

From the four assorted red print fat quarters:

- Cut a **total** of 28 **rectangles E** 1½" x 2½".
- Cut a **total** of 28 **rectangles F** 1½" x 4½".
- Cut a **total** of 28 **rectangles G** 1½" x 6½".

From the two assorted black print fat quarters:

- Cut a **total** of 18 **rectangles E** 1½" x 2½".
- Cut a **total** of 18 **rectangles F** 1½" x 4½".
- Cut a **total** of 18 **rectangles G** 1½" x 6½".

From black medium scale floral print fat quarter:

- Cut 4 **squares A** 4½" x 4½".

From black and red floral print fat quarter:

- Cut 4 **squares A** 4½" x 4½".
- Cut 2 **rectangles E** 1½" x 2½".
- Cut 2 **rectangles F** 1½" x 4½".
- Cut 2 **rectangles G** 1½" x 6½".

From black, red, and white print fat quarter:

- Cut 4 **squares A** 4½" x 4½".
- Cut 2 **rectangles E** 1½" x 2½".
- Cut 2 **rectangles F** 1½" x 4½".
- Cut 2 **rectangles G** 1½" x 6½".

From ivory and black print fabric:

- Cut 15 **squares D** 2½" x 2½ ".

From ivory print fabric:

- Cut 7 strips 1½" wide. From these strips, cut 180 **squares H** 1½" x 1½".

From red and black stripe fabric:

- Cut 6 strips 2½" wide. From these strips, cut 16 **rectangles B** 2½" x 4½", 16 **rectangles C** 2½" x 8½", and 4 **corner squares** 2½" x 2½".
- Cut 1 strip 1½" wide. From this strip, cut 2 **rectangles E** 1½" x 2½", 2 **rectangles F** 1½" x 4½", and 2 rectangles G 1½" x 6½".

From black and red stripe fabric:

- Cut 6 strips 2½" wide. From these strips, cut 14 **rectangles B** 2½" x 4½" and 14 **rectangles C** 2½" x 8½".

From ivory and red print fabric:

- Cut 5 strips 2½" wide. Piece these strips together end to end. From this strip, cut 2 **inner side borders #1** 2½" x 48½" and 2 **inner top/bottom borders #1** 2½" x 40½".

From black and ivory trailing floral fabric:

- Cut 8 strips 4½" wide. Piece these strips together end to end. From this strip, cut 2 **outer side borders #2** 4½" x 75" and 2 **outer top/bottom borders #2** 4½" x 67".
- Cut 2 strips 1½" wide. From these strips, cut 4 **rectangles E** 1½" x 2½", 4 **rectangles F** 1½" x 4½", and 4 **rectangles G** 1½" x 6½".

From floral trellis print fabric:

- Cut 3 **squares A** 4½" x 4½".
- Cut 8 strips 1½" wide. Piece these strips together end to end. From this strip, cut 2 **outer side borders #3** 1½" x 75" and 2 **outer top/bottom borders #3** 1½" x 67".

From black, red, and tan small print fabric:

- Cut 8 strips 5½" wide. Piece these strips together end to end. From this strip, cut 2 **outer side borders #4** 5½" x 75" and 2 **outer top/bottom borders #4** 5½" x 67".

From black and ivory stripe fabric:

- Cut 2 strips 1½" wide. From these strips, cut 4 **rectangles E** 1½" x 2½", 4 **rectangles F** 1½" x 4½", and 4 **rectangles G** 1½" x 6½".
- Cut 8 binding strips 2¼" wide.

PREPARING FUSIBLE APPLIQUÉS

Appliqué patterns, *page 44-45, do not include seam allowances. Follow* ***Preparing Fusible Appliqués,*** *page 59, to cut out appliqués.*

From assorted red print fat quarters:

- Cut a **total** of 6 **flowers J**.
- Cut a **total** of 8 **circle flower centers M**.

From black medium scale floral print fat quarter:

- Cut 6 **flower centers K**.

From ivory and black print fat quarter:

- Cut 12 **leaves N**.
- Cut 12 **leaves N** in reverse.

From ivory and red print fabric:

- Cut 8 **circle flowers L**.

MAKING THE FRAMED SQUARE BLOCKS

*Follow **Machine Piecing,** page 56, and **Pressing,** page 57, to make quilt top. Use ¼" seam allowances throughout.*

1. Sew a red **rectangle B** to opposite sides of a black **square A**. Press seam allowances away from **square A**. Sew a red **rectangle C** to the top and bottom. Make a **total** of 8 **Framed Square Block A's**.

Framed Square Block A (make 8)

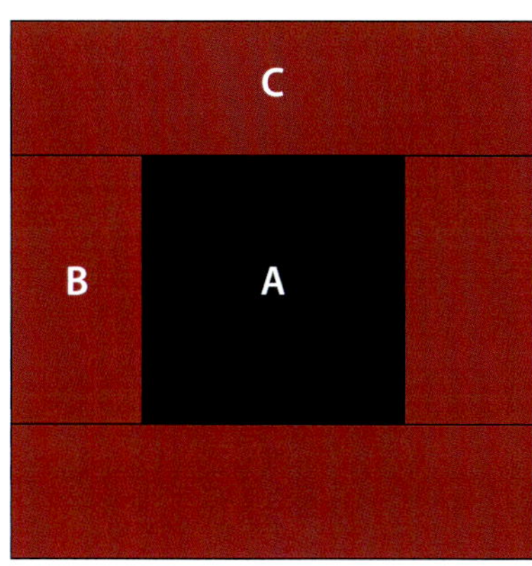

2. Using black **squares A** and black **rectangles B and C**, make 7 **Framed Square Block B's**.

Framed Square Block B (make 7)

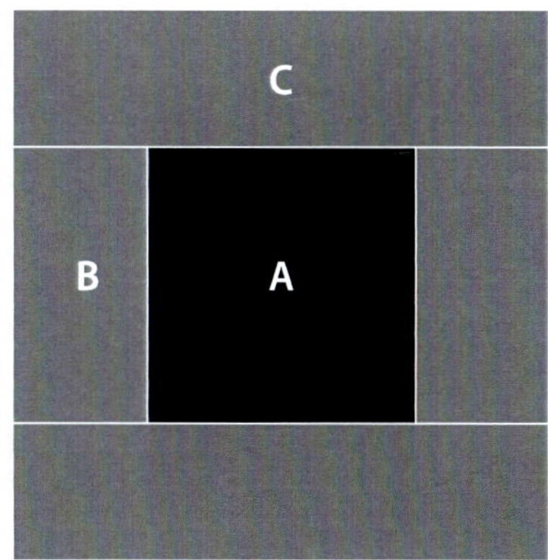

MAKING THE NIGHT CROSSING BLOCKS

1. Referring to the **Night Crossing Block**, randomly arrange pieces D through H for a scrappy look. Notice that half of the block contains black fabrics and half of the block contains red fabrics.

2. Sew a **rectangle E** to opposite sides of a **square D**. Press the seam allowances toward the darker fabric.

3. Sew a **square H** to opposite short ends of a **rectangle E**. Make 2. Press the seam allowances toward the darker fabric. Sew these to the top and bottom of the unit made in Step 2.

4. Continue adding rectangles and squares in this manner to make the **Night Crossing Block**. Make a total of 15 **Night Crossing Blocks**.

Night Crossing Block (make 15)

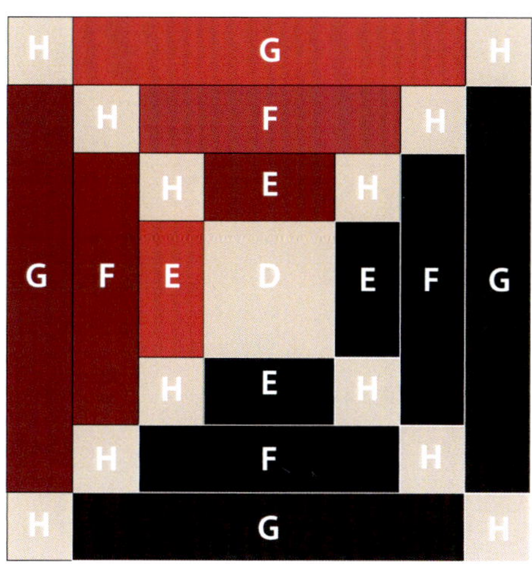

ASSEMBLING THE QUILT TOP

*Refer to **Quilt Top,** page 45, to assemble quilt top.*

Inner Borders

1. Alternating the blocks, sew the blocks together in rows. Sew the rows together.

2. Sew the **inner side border #1's** to the quilt top. Sew a **corner square** to the short ends of the **inner top/ bottom border** #1's to quilt top. Press the seam allowances toward the ivory and red print fabric.

3. Sew the **inner top/bottom border #1's** to the quilt top.

Outer Borders

1. For **outer side border**, match the centers and sew 1 **outer side border #2**, 1 **outer side border #3**, and 1 **outer side border #4** together. Press the seam allowances toward the narrow border strip. Make 2 **outer side borders.**

2. Repeat Step 1 using **outer top/bottom borders** to make 2 **outer top/bottom borders**.

3. Referring to **Quilt Top** for placement, position appliqués on border and fuse in place. Follow **Satin Stitch Appliqué,** page 59, to add appliqués to quilt top. Note that you will not be able to position the corner flowers until after the borders are sewn to the quilt.

4. Refer to **Adding Mitered Borders,** page 62, to add outer side, top, and bottom borders to quilt top.

5. Fuse and appliqué the corner flowers on the borders.

COMPLETING THE QUILT

1. Follow **Quilting,** page 63, to mark, layer, and quilt as desired. Quilt shown is quilted in the ditch along each border and with a feather design in the quilt top center and in each wide border. There is meandering quilting in the inner borders.

2. Follow **Making a Hanging Sleeve,** page 65, if a hanging sleeve is desired.

3. Sew **binding strips** together end to end diagonally. Follow **Attaching Binding with Mitered Corners,** page 66, to bind quilt.

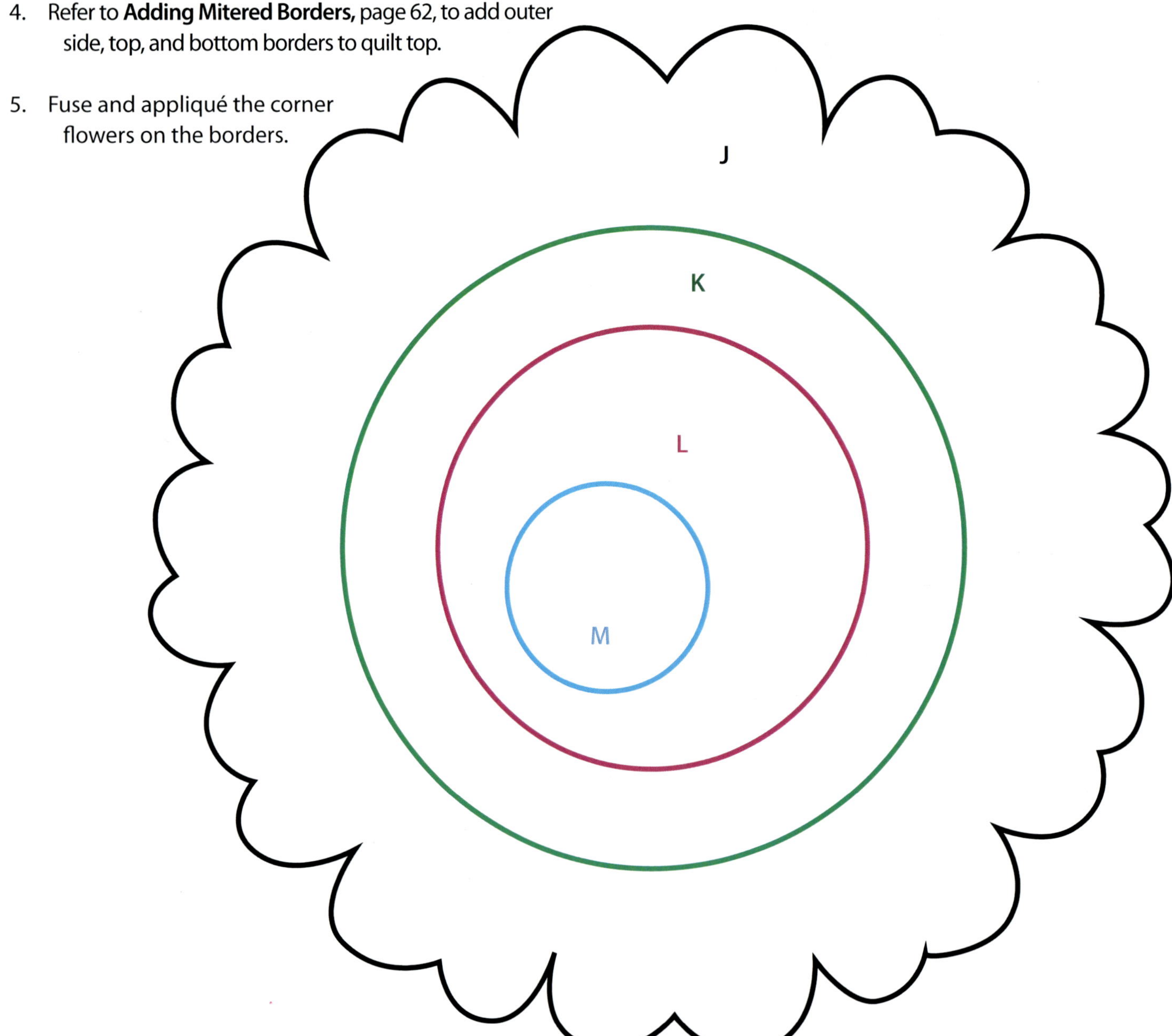

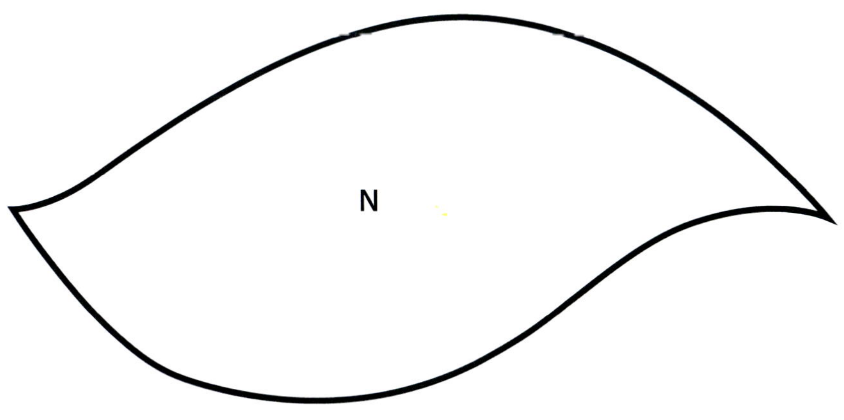

Quilt Top

Glory Days

Finished Quilt Size: 88" x 88" (224 cm x 224 cm)
Finished Block Size: 16" x 16" (41 cm x 41 cm)

SHOPPING LIST

Yardage is based on 43"/44" (109 cm/112 cm) wide fabric with a usable width of 40" (102 cm). Fat quarters are approximately 22" x 18" (56 cm x 46 cm).

- ☐ 1 fat quarter of red and cream paisley print fabric for appliqués
- ☐ 1 fat quarter of light blue print fabric for appliqués
- ☐ ¾ yd (69 cm) of blue cable stripe fabric for appliqué vine
- ☐ ½ yd (46 cm) of blue and cream paisley print fabric for blocks and appliqués
- ☐ ½ yd (46 cm) of blue and cream plaid print fabric for blocks and appliqués
- ☐ ⅝ yd (57 cm) of navy paisley print fabric for blocks and appliqués
- ☐ ¾ yd (69 cm) of pink print fabric for blocks and appliqués
- ☐ 1⅜ yds (1.3 m) of red cable stripe fabric for appliqués and binding
- ☐ 1¼ yds (1.1 m) of red and pink print fabric for blocks and appliqués
- ☐ 1⅜ yds (1.3 m) of dark red print fabric for blocks and borders
- ☐ 1½ yds (1.4 m) of navy print fabric for blocks and borders
- ☐ 4¾ yds (4.3 m) of cream and red print fabric for background
- ☐ 8 yds (7.3 m) of fabric for backing
- ☐ freezer paper - 1 strip 10" x 82"
- ☐ template plastic for Needle-Turn Applique´ **or** paper-backed fusible web for Machine Appliqué
- ☐ ½" (12 mm) bias press bar
- ☐ 96" x 96" (244 cm x 244 cm) piece of batting

CUTTING THE PIECES

Follow ***Rotary Cutting,*** *page 55, to cut fabric. Cut all strips from the selvage-to-selvage width of the fabric. Cut strips from fat quarters parallel to the long edge. The borders are cut longer than needed and will be trimmed to fit quilt top center. All measurements include ¼" seam allowances*

From blue and cream paisley print fabric:

- Cut 3 strips 2½" wide. From these strips, cut 32 **squares A** 2½" x 2½"

From blue and cream plaid print fabric:

- Cut 5 strips 2½" wide. From these strips, cut 72 **squares A** 2½" x 2½".

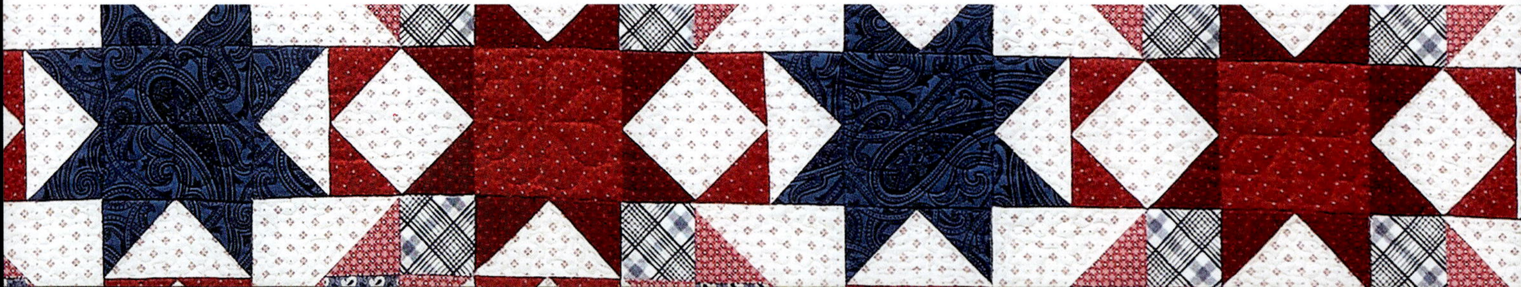

From navy paisley print fabric:

- Cut 2 strips 4½" wide. From these strips, cut 13 **squares C** 4½" x 4½".
- Cut 2 strips 2½" wide. From these strips, cut 48 **squares A** 2½" x 2½".

From pink print fabric:

- Cut 6 strips 2⅞" wide. From these strips, cut 72 squares 2⅞" x 2⅞". Cut each square in half *once* diagonally to make 144 **triangles B**.

From red cable stripe fabric:

- Cut square for bias vine 24" x 24".
- Cut 9 binding strips 2¼" wide.

From red and pink print fabric:

- Cut 8 strips 2½" wide. From these strips, cut 120 **squares A** 2½" x 2½".
- Cut 2 strips 4½" wide. From these strips, cut 12 **squares C** 4½" x 4½".
- Cut 1 strip 3½" wide. From this strip, cut 4 **squares F** 3½" x 3½".

From dark red print fabric:

- Cut 8 strips 2½" wide. From these strips, cut 120 **squares A** 2½" x 2½".
- Cut 6 **inner border strips** 3½" wide.

From navy print fabric:

- Cut 5 strips 2½" wide. From these strips, cut 72 **squares A** 2½" x 2½".
- Cut 8 **outer border strips** 3½" wide.
- Cut 1 strip 3½" wide. From this strip, cut 4 **squares F** 3½" x 3½".

From cream and red print fabric:

- Cut 4 ***lengthwise*** **borders** 10½" x 83½".
- Cut 7 strips 2½" wide. From this strip, cut 60 **rectangles D** 2½" x 4½".
- Cut 7 strips 4½" wide. From these strips, cut 60 **squares C** 4½" x 4½".
- Cut 5 strips 4⅞" wide. From these strips, cut 36 squares 4⅞" x 4⅞". Cut each square in half *once* diagonally to make 72 **triangles E**.

CUTTING THE APPLIQUÉS

You can hand or machine appliqué the vine, flowers and leaves. Use patterns, page 54, and follow ***Making and Using Templates,*** *page 58, for hand appliqué* ***or*** *follow* ***Preparing Fusible Appliqués,*** *page 59, for machine appliqué.*

From red and cream paisley print fabric:

- Cut 4 **flower centers.**
- Cut 16 **leaves.**

From light blue print fabric:

- Cut 16 **leaves.**

From blue cable stripe fabric:

- Cut **square for bias vine** 23" x 23".
- Cut 5 **leaves.**

From blue and cream paisley print fabric:

- Cut 8 **flower centers.**
- Cut 16 **leaves.**

From blue and cream plaid print fabric:

- Cut 15 **leaves.**

From navy paisley print fabric:

- Cut 4 **flowers.**

From pink print fabric:

- Cut 14 **leaves.**

From red cable stripe fabric:

- Cut **rectangle for bias vine** 13" x 31".
- Cut 7 **leaves.**

From red and pink print fabric:

- Cut 8 **flowers.**
- Cut 9 **leaves.**

MAKING THE BLOCKS

Follow ***Machine Piecing****, page 56, and* ***Pressing****, page 57, to make the quilt top. Use ¼" seam allowances throughout.*

1. Referring to **Fig. 1** and pressing the seam allowances toward the pink triangles, sew 2 blue & cream plaid **square A's**, 4 pink **triangle B's**, and 1 blue and cream paisley **square A** together to make **Unit 1**. Make a total of 36. Press the seam allowances toward the pink triangles.

Fig. 1

Unit 1 (make 36)

2. Finger press 2 cream and red **triangles E** in the center of the long side to mark the center. Matching the centers, sew 1 **triangle E** to opposite sides of **Unit 1** to make **Unit 2**. Press the seam allowances toward the **triangles E**. Make a total of 36.

Unit 2 (make 36)

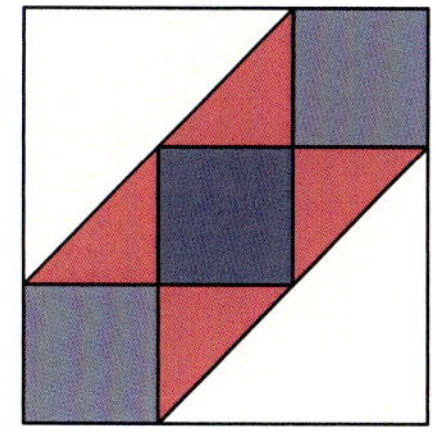

3. Draw a diagonal line on the wrong side of each red and pink **square A** and each navy **square A**. Place 1 red and pink **square A** on 1 corner of a cream and red **square C**. Stitch on the drawn line ***(Fig. 2)***. Trim seam allowance to ¼" ***(Fig. 3)*** and press open.

Fig. 2

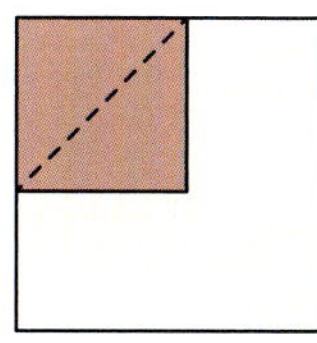

Fig. 3

In the same manner, add another red and pink **square A** to 1 adjacent corner, then add a navy **square A** to each remaining corner ***(Fig. 4)*** to make **Unit 3**. Make 36 **Unit 3's**.

Fig. 4

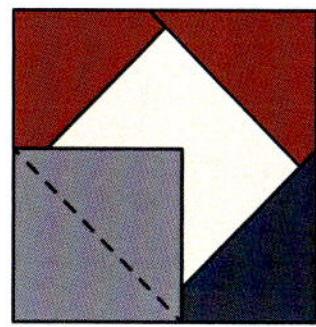

Unit 3 (make 36)

4. Draw a diagonal line on the wrong side of 72 dark red **squares A**. Place 1 dark red **square A** on 1 corner of a cream and red **rectangle D**. Stitch on the drawn line ***(Fig. 5)***. trim seam allowance to ¼" ***(Fig. 6)*** and press open. Repeat with another dark red **square A** on opposite corner to make **Unit 4**. Make 36 **Unit 4's**.

Fig. 5

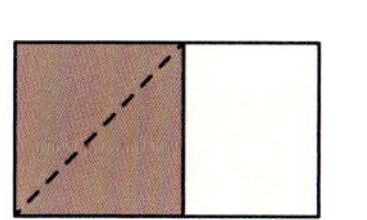

Fig. 6

Unit 4 (make 36)

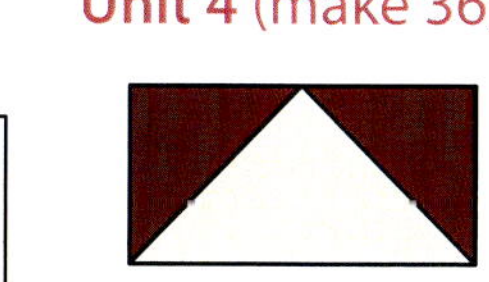

5. Sew 1 **Unit 3** and 1 **Unit 4** together to make **Unit 5**. Press the seam allowances toward the **Unit 2**. Make 36 **Unit 5's**.

Unit 5 (make 36)

6. Pressing seam allowances in directions indicated by arrows, sew 4 **Unit 1's**, 4 **Unit 5's**, and 1 navy **square C** into rows. Sew rows together to make a **Block**. Make 9 **Blocks**.

Block (make 9)

MAKING THE SASHINGS

1. Using the same construction method that you used to construct a **Unit 3**, use 48 red and pink **squares A**, 48 dark red **squares A**, and 24 cream and red **squares C** to make 24 **Unit 6's**.

Unit 6 (make 24)

2. Using the same construction method that you used to construct a **Unit 4**, use 48 navy **squares A** and 24 cream and red **rectangles D** to make 24 **Unit 7's**.

Unit 7 (make 24)

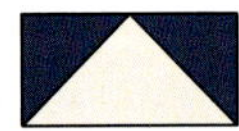

3. Sew 1 **Unit 6** and 1 **Unit 7** together to make **Unit 8**. Press the seam allowances toward the **Unit 5**. Make a total of 36 **Unit 7's**.

Unit 8 (make 36)

4. Sew 2 **Unit 8's** and 1 red and pink **square C** together to make a **Sashing**. Make 12 **Sashings**.

Sashing (make 12)

ASSEMBLING THE QUILT TOP

*Refer to **Assembly Diagram,** to assemble the quilt top center.*

1. Sew 3 **Blocks** and 2 **sashings** together to make a **block row**. Make 3 block rows.

2. Sew 3 **Blocks** and 2 navy paisley squares together to make a **sashing row.** Make 2 **sashing rows.**

3. Sew **Block** and **sashing rows** together to make the **quilt top center.**

Assembly Diagram

Inner Border

1. For the **inner border**, sew the dark red 3½" wide strips together end-to-end to make one **continuous inner border strip**. Cut 4 **inner borders** 56½" long from the **inner border strip**. Matching centers and corner, sew the side **inner borders** to the **quilt top center**. Press the seam allowances toward the borders.

2. Sew a navy **square F** to the ends of the remaining 2 borders. Press the seam allowances toward the border. Sew borders to the top and bottom of the **quilt top center**. Press the seam allowances toward the borders.

Appliqué Border

*Follow **Needle-Turn Appliqué,** page 58, or **Machine Appliqué,** page 59, to add the leaves and flowers (patterns on page 54).*

1. Use red **bias binding square**, follow **Making a Continuous Bias Strip,** page 65, to make a 1½" wide bias strip.

2. Matching wrong sides, fold strip in half and stitch ½" from fold forming a tube; trim seam allowance to ⅛". Press tube flat, centering seam allowance on back so raw edge isn't visible from front. Using ½" bias bar makes pressing faster and easier. Cut tube in half to make two vines.

3. Repeat Steps 1-2 using blue **bias binding square**.

4. Cut a strip of freezer paper 10" x 82". Create center registration lines by folding borders in half *lengthwise* and horizontally; crease firmly.

5. Referring to **Vine Placement Diagram**, mark 8" from either side of the center and crease. Repeat twice in each direction. On the outside edge of the center line, measure in 3" and mark (red mark on Diagram). At the first 8" increment from the center, measure in 3" from the inside edge and mark. Repeat this process 2 more times, referring to **Diagram E.** Repeat for the remaining end of the guide. On the dull side of the freezer paper, use a black pen or marker to draw a gentle curve to connect the marks.

Vine Placement Diagram

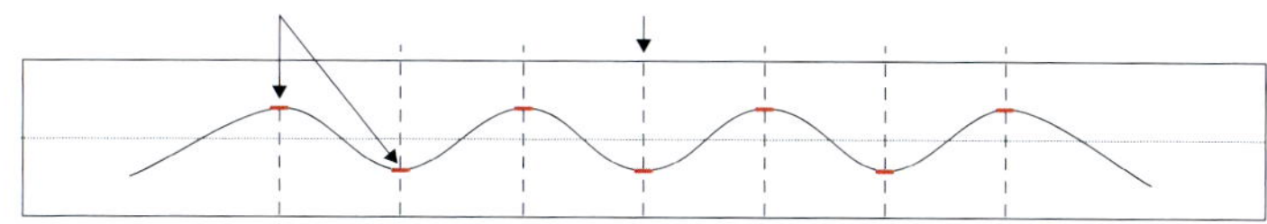

6. Center a cream **border strip** on top of the placement guide; pin. You should be able to see the placement guide through the fabric. Position the vine and baste in place with pins or small drops of fabric glue.

   Note: If you press the vine with a little steam as you are positioning it will bend smoothly and lie flat. Leaving about 12"-14" of vine unsewn at each end (vine ends will be attached after borders are sewn to quilt top), stitch vine in place by hand or machine. Pin loose vine ends out of the way of all seam allowances.

7. Referring to the **Border Diagram**, position flowers, flower centers, and leaves on a border. Do not place the last 2-3 leaves on each end of the border. These will be added after the borders are attached to the quilt top. Stitch in place by hand or machine. Make a total of 4 borders.

Border Diagram

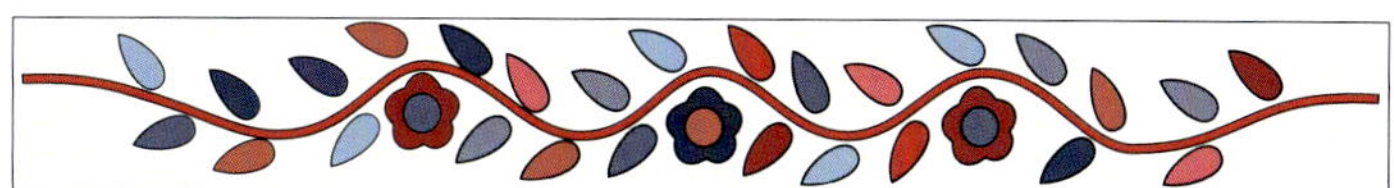

8. Mark the center of each long edge of the quilt top and the center of each border. Match center marks and sew the borders to the quilt, stopping stitching ¼" from the ends. Miter the corners ***(Figs. 7-8)***.

Fig. 7

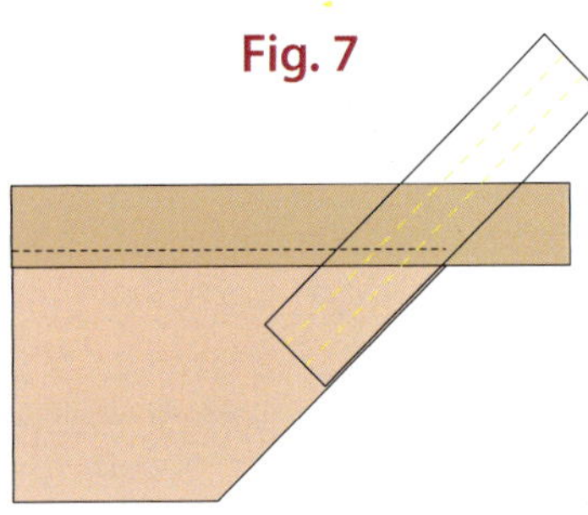

Fig. 8

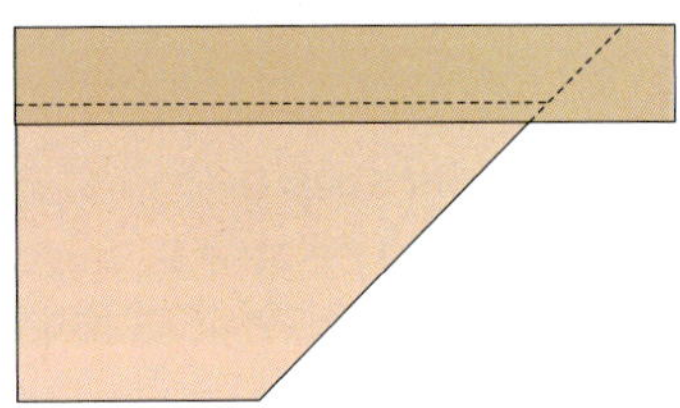

9. Position **vine ends**, overlapping them in the corners. Turning under the raw ends, stitch vines in place. Appliqué the remaining leaves in place.

Outer Border

1. For the outer border, sew the navy 3½" wide strips together end-to-end to make one **continuous inner border strip**. Cut 4 **outer borders** 82½" long from the **outer border strip**. Matching centers and corner, sew the **side outer borders** to the **quilt top center**. Press the seam allowances toward the borders.

2. Sew a pink and red **square F** to the ends of the remaining 2 borders. Press the seam allowances toward the border. Sew borders to the top and bottom of the quilt top center. Press the seam allowances toward the borders.

COMPLETING THE QUILT

1. Follow **Quilting,** page 63, to mark, layer, and quilt as desired. Quilt shown has feather quilting in the narrow borders and meander quilting in the appliqué border. The blocks are outline quilted around the stars and have meander quilting in the light background areas. The appliqués are outline quilted.

2. Follow **Making a Hanging Sleeve,** page 65, if a hanging sleeve is desired.

3. Use **binding strips** and follow **Binding,** page 66, to bind quilt.

Quilt Top

Glory Days

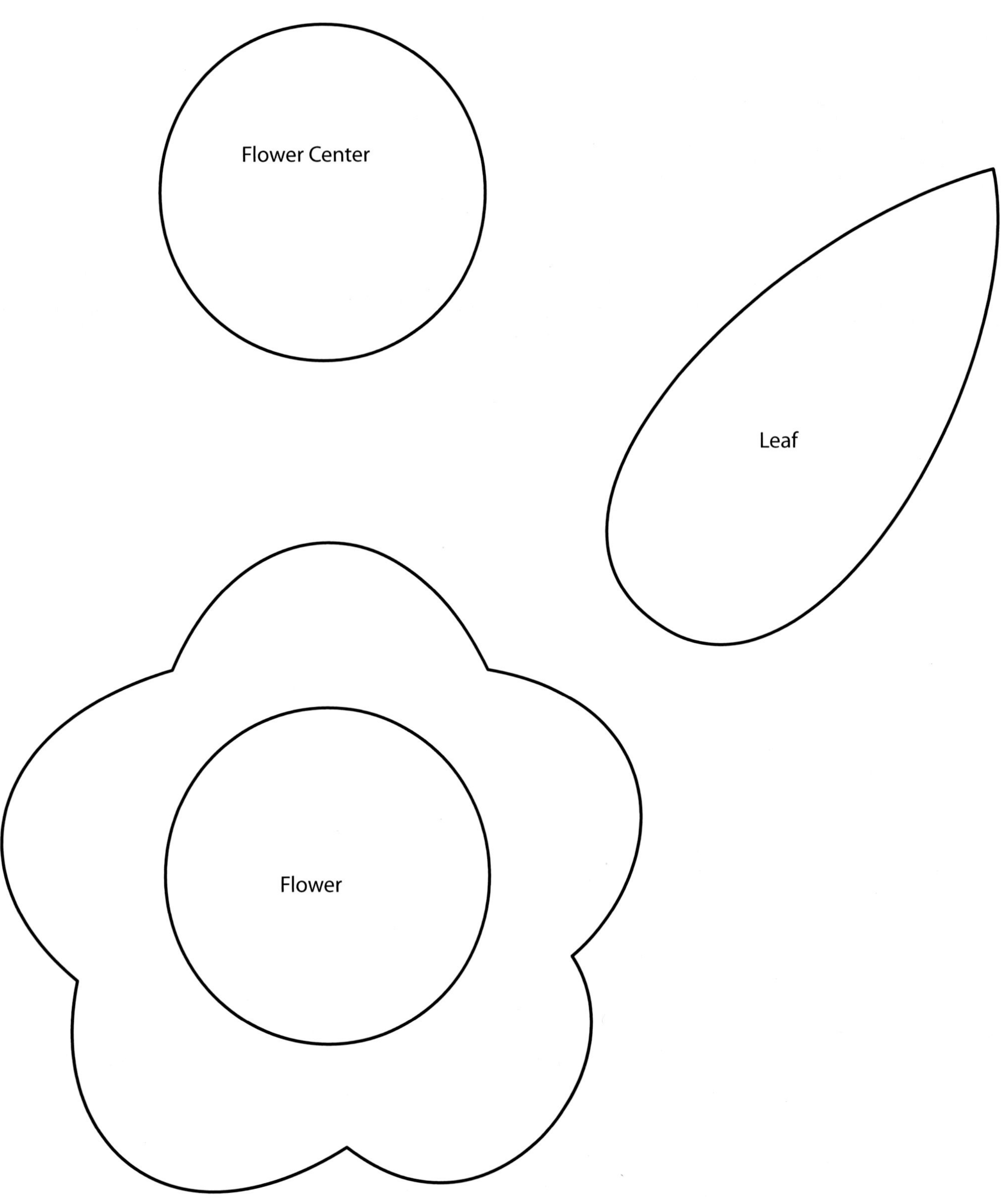

General Instructions

To make your quilting easier and more enjoyable, we encourage you to carefully read all of the general instructions, study the color photographs, and familiarize yourself with the individual project instructions before beginning a project.

FABRICS

SELECTING FABRICS

Choose high-quality, medium-weight 100% cotton fabrics. All-cotton fabrics hold a crease better, fray less, and are easier to quilt than cotton/polyester blends.

Yardage requirements listed for each project are based on 43"/44" wide fabric with a "usable" width of 40" after shrinkage and trimming selvages. Actual usable width will probably vary slightly from fabric to fabric. Our recommended yardage lengths should be adequate for occasional re-squaring of fabric when many cuts are required.

PREPARING FABRICS

Pre-washing fabrics may cause edges to ravel. As a result, your pre-cut fabric pieces may not be large enough to cut all of the pieces required for your chosen project. Therefore, we do not recommend pre-washing your yardage or pre-cut fabrics.

Before cutting, prepare fabrics with a steam iron set on cotton and starch or sizing. The starch or sizing will give the fabric a crisp finish. This will make cutting more accurate and may make piecing easier.

ROTARY CUTTING

CUTTING FROM YARDAGE

- Place fabric on work surface with fold closest to you.
- Cut all strips from the selvage-to-selvage width of the fabric.
- Square left edge of fabric using rotary cutter and rulers ***(Figs. 1 - 2)***.

Fig. 1

Fig. 2

- To cut each strip required for a project, place ruler over cut edge of fabric, aligning desired marking on ruler with cut edge; make cut ***(Fig. 3)***.

Fig. 3

- When cutting several strips from a single piece of fabric, it is important to make sure that cuts remain at a perfect right angle to the fold; square fabric as needed.

CUTTING FROM FAT QUARTERS OR FAT EIGHTHS

- Place fabric flat on work surface with lengthwise (short) edge closest to you.
- Cut all strips parallel to the long edge of the fabric in the same manner as cutting from yardage.
- To cut each strip required for a project, place ruler over cut edge of fabric, aligning desired marking on ruler with cut edge; make cut.

MACHINE PIECING

Precise cutting, followed by accurate piecing, will ensure that all pieces of quilt top fit together well.

- Set sewing machine stitch length for approximately 11 stitches per inch.
- Use neutral-colored general-purpose sewing thread (not quilting thread) in needle and in bobbin.
- An accurate ¼" seam allowance is essential. Presser feet that are ¼" wide are available for most sewing machines.
- When piecing, always place pieces right sides together and match raw edges; pin if necessary.
- Chain piecing saves time and will usually result in more accurate piecing.
- Trim away points of seam allowances that extend beyond edges of sewn pieces.

SEWING STRIP SETS

When there are several strips to assemble into a strip set, first sew strips together into pairs, then sew pairs together to form strip set. To help avoid distortion, sew seams in opposite directions ***(Fig. 4)***.

Fig. 4

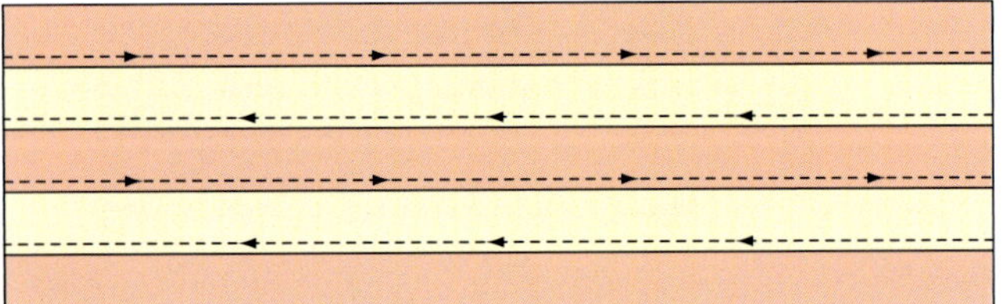

SEWING ACROSS SEAM INTERSECTIONS

When sewing across intersection of two seams, place pieces right sides together and match seams exactly, making sure seam allowances are pressed in opposite directions ***(Fig. 5)***.

Fig. 5

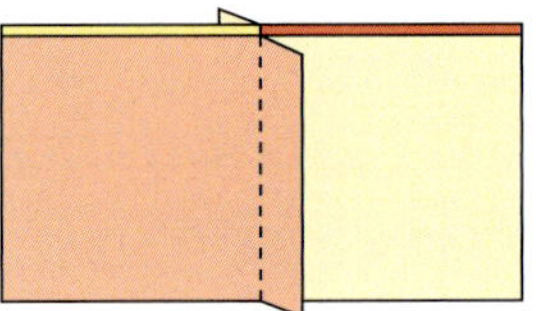

SEWING SHARP POINTS

To ensure sharp points when joining triangular or diagonal pieces, stitch across the center of the "X" (shown in pink) formed on wrong side by previous seams ***(Fig. 6)***.

Fig. 6

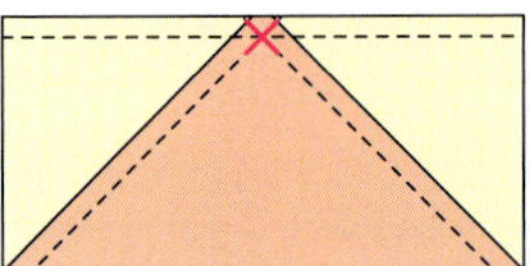

FOUNDATION PAPER PIECING

1. Projects involving paper piecing will provide a foundation pattern. Photocopy pattern the number of times indicated in the project instructions.

2. Using neutral-colored thread, follow numerical order to place and sew fabrics.

3. With wrong sides together, cover area 1 of foundation with fabric for area 1. Pin fabric in place. Fold foundation on line between area 1 and area 2 ***(Fig. 7)***. Trim fabric ¼" from fold. Unfold foundation.

Fig. 7

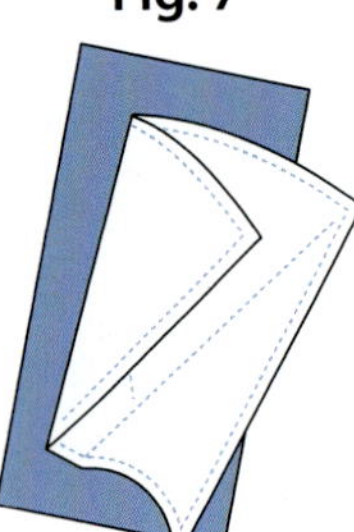

4. Matching right sides and trimmed edges, place fabric piece #2 on fabric piece #1 ***(Fig. 8)***, making sure fabric extends beyond outer edges of area 2. Turn foundation over to front and pin.

Fig. 8

5. Sew along line between areas 1 and 2, extending sewing a few stitches beyond beginning and end of line ***(Fig. 9)***.

Fig. 9

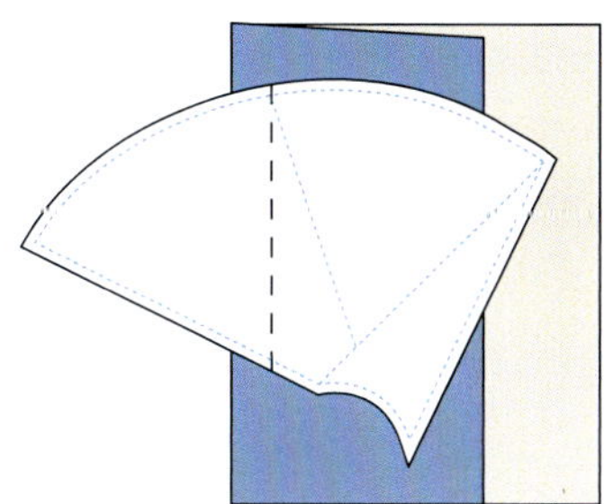

6. Open out piece #2; press.
Pin piece #2 to foundation ***(Fig. 10)***.

Fig. 10

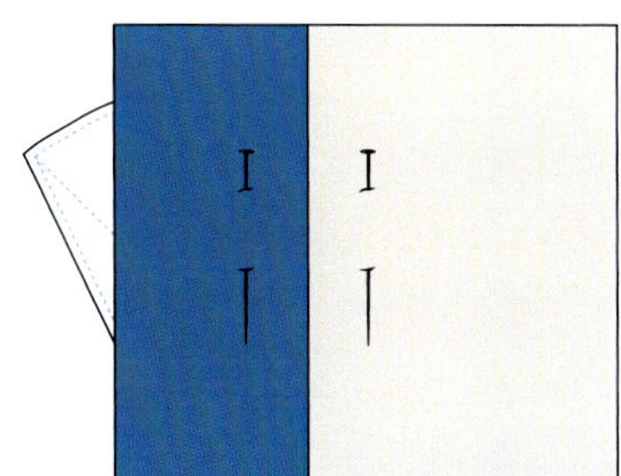

7. Continue adding pieces in same manner in numerical order until foundation is covered.

8. Trim fabric and foundation along outer lines to complete block. Carefully remove paper foundation.

PRESSING

- Use steam iron set on "Cotton' for all pressing.
- Press after sewing each seam.
- Seam allowances are almost always pressed to one side, usually toward darker fabric. However, to reduce bulk it may occasionally be necessary to press seam allowances toward the lighter fabric or even to press them open.
- To prevent dark fabric seam allowance from showing through light fabric, trim darker seam allowance slightly narrower than lighter seam allowance.
- To press long seams, such as those in long strip sets, without curving or other distortion, lay strips across width of the ironing board.

NEEDLE-TURN APPLIQUÉ

MAKING AND USING TEMPLATES

Needle-Turn Appliqué template patterns do not include seam allowances.

1. To make a template from a pattern, use a permanent fine-point pen to carefully trace pattern onto template plastic, making sure to transfer any alignment and grainline markings. Cut out template along inner edge of drawn line. Check template against original pattern for accuracy.

2. If using an appliqué template, place template on right side of appliqué fabric. Lightly draw around template with pencil, leaving at least 1" between shapes. Repeat for number of shapes specified in project instructions. Cut out shapes approximately 3/16" outside drawn line. Clip inside curves and points to but not through drawn line.

NEEDLE-TURN APPLIQUÉ

Using your needle to turn under the seam allowance while blindstitching (page 68) an appliqué piece to the background fabric is called "needle-turn" appliqué.

1. Arrange shapes on background fabric and pin or baste in place.

2. Thread a sharps needle with a single strand of general-purpose sewing thread that matches appliqué; knot one end.

3. Begin blindstitching on as straight an edge as possible, turning a small section of 3/16" seam allowance to wrong side with needle, concealing drawn line ***(Fig. 11)***. Clip curves as needed, up to but not through drawn line.

Fig. 11

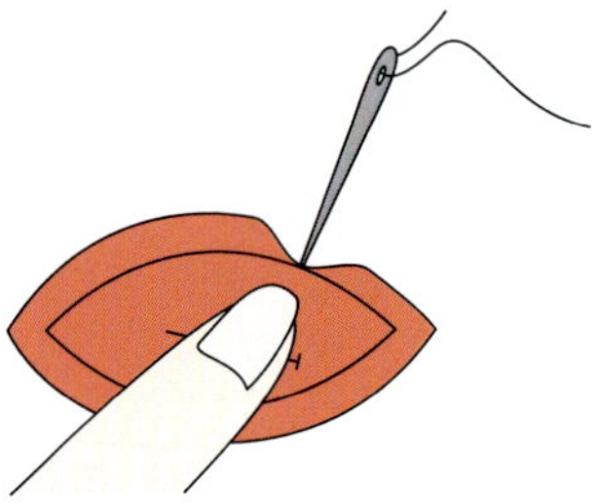

4. To stitch outward points, stitch to ½" from point ***(Fig. 12)***. Turn seam allowance under at point ***(Fig. 13)***; then turn remainder of seam allowance between stitching and point. Stitch to point, taking two or three stitches at top of point to secure. Turn under small amount of seam allowance past point and resume stitching.

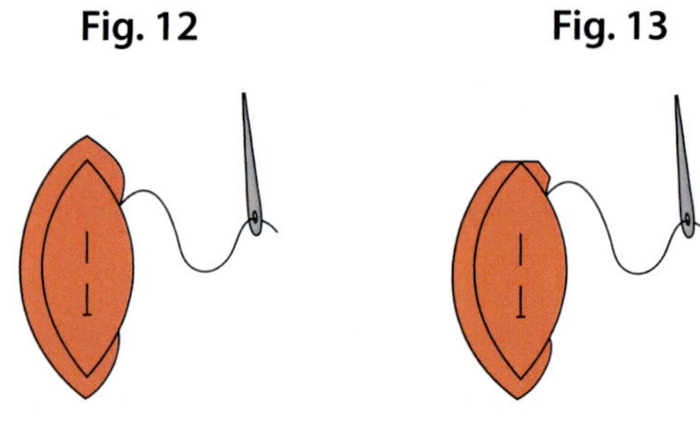

Fig. 12 **Fig. 13**

5. To stitch inward point, stitch to ½" from point ***(Fig. 14)***. Clip to but not through seam allowance at point ***(Fig. 15)***. Turn seam allowance under between stitching and point. Stitch to point, taking two or three stitches at point to secure. Turn under small amount of seam allowance past point and resume stitching.

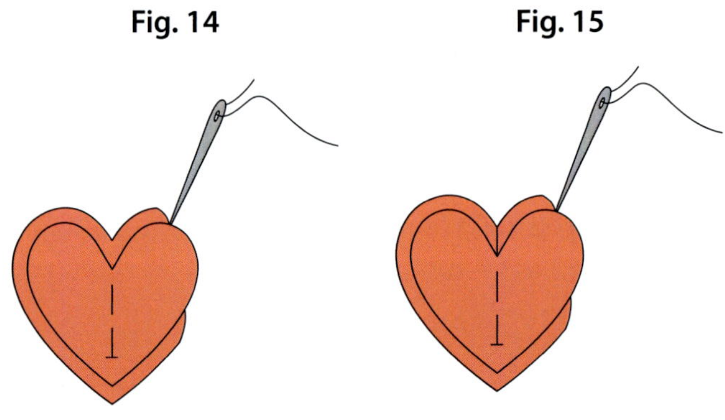

Fig. 14 **Fig. 15**

6. Do not turn under or stitch seam allowances that will be covered by other appliqué pieces.

7. For appliqué pieces that are layered (such as a flower center on top of a flower), appliqué top piece to bottom piece before appliquéing bottom piece to background.

8. To appliqué pressed bias strips, baste strips in place and blindstitch along edges.

9. To reduce bulk, background fabric behind appliqués may be cut away. After stitching appliqués in place, turn background over and use sharp scissors or specially designed appliqué scissors to trim away background fabric approximately ¼" from stitching line. Take care not to cut appliqué fabric or stitches. Bulk may be reduced behind layered appliqués by cutting away bottom layer of appliqués.

MACHINE APPLIQUÉ

PREPARING FUSIBLE APPLIQUÉS

White or light-colored fabrics may need to be lined with fusible interfacing before applying fusible web to prevent darker fabrics from showing through.

1. Place paper-backed fusible web, paper side up, over appliqué pattern. Trace pattern onto paper side of web with pencil as many times as indicated in project instructions for a single fabric. To reverse a pattern, use a black fine-point marker to trace the pattern onto plain white paper. Flip the paper over and trace the pattern onto the paper side of the fusible web from the "wrong" side of the plain white paper.

2. Follow manufacturer's instructions to fuse traced patterns to wrong side of fabrics. Do not remove paper backing.

3. Use scissors to cut out appliqué pieces along traced lines. Remove paper backing from all pieces.

SATIN STITCH APPLIQUÉ

A good satin stitch is a thick, smooth, almost solid line of zigzag stitching that covers the exposed raw edges of appliqué pieces.

1. Pin stabilizer, such as paper or any of the commercially available products, on wrong side of background fabric before stitching appliqués in place.

2. Thread sewing machine with general-purpose thread; use general-purpose thread that matches background fabric in bobbin.

3. Set sewing machine for a medium (approximately ⅛") zigzag stitch and a short stitch length. Slightly loosening the top tension may yield a smoother stitch.

4. Begin by stitching two or three stitches in place (drop feed dogs or set stitch length at 0) to anchor thread. Most of the Satin Stitch should be on the appliqué with the right edge of the stitch falling at the outside edge of the appliqué. Stitch over all exposed raw edges of appliqué pieces.

5. (Note: Dots on ***Figs. 16 – 21*** indicate where to leave needle in fabric when pivoting.) For outside corners, stitch just past corner, stopping with needle in background fabric ***(Fig. 16)***. Raise presser foot. Pivot project, lower presser foot, and stitch adjacent side ***(Fig. 17)***.

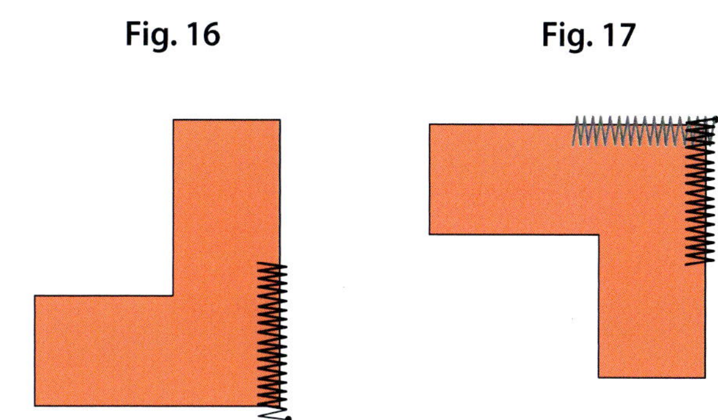
Fig. 16 **Fig. 17**

6. For inside corners, stitch just past corner, stopping with needle in appliqué fabric ***(Fig. 18)***. Raise presser foot. Pivot project, lower presser foot, and stitch adjacent side ***(Fig. 19)***.

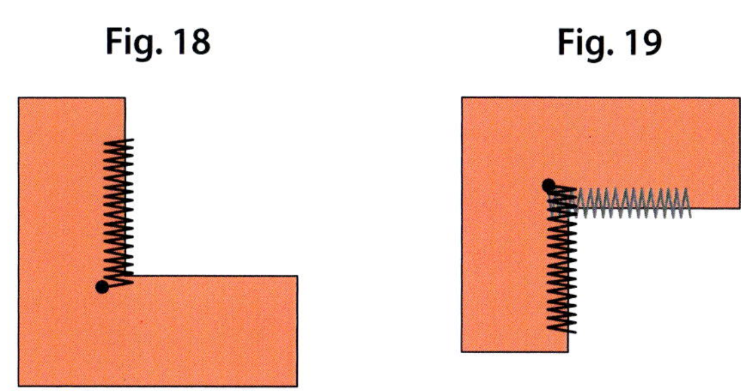
Fig. 18 **Fig. 19**

7. When stitching outside curves, stop with needle in background fabric. Raise presser foot and pivot project as needed. Lower presser foot and continue stitching, pivoting as often as necessary to follow curve ***(Fig. 20)***.

Fig. 20

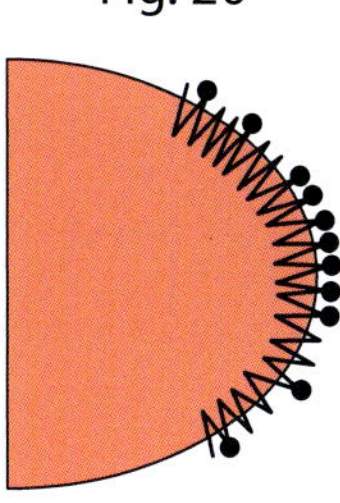

8. When stitching inside curves, stop with needle in appliqué fabric. Raise presser foot and pivot project as needed. Lower presser foot and continue stitching, pivoting as often as necessary to follow curve ***(Fig. 21)***.

Fig. 21

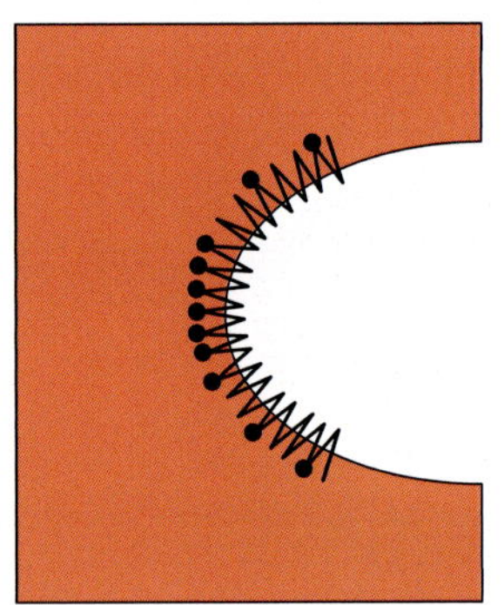

9. Do not backstitch at end of stitching. Pull threads to wrong side of background fabric; knot thread and trim ends.

10. Carefully tear away stabilizer.

BLANKET STITCH APPLIQUÉ

Some sewing machines are capable of a Blanket Stitch. Refer to your owner's manual for machine set-up. If your machine does not have this stitch, try any of the decorative stitches your machine has until you are satisfied with the look.

1. Thread sewing machine and bobbin with 100% cotton thread in desired weight.

2. Attach an open-toe presser foot. Select far right needle position and needle down (if your machine has these features).

3. If desired, pin a stabilizer, such as paper or any of the commercially available products, on wrong side of background fabric before stitching appliqués in place.

4. Bring bobbin thread to the top of the fabric by lowering then raising the needle, bringing up the bobbin thread loop. Pull the loop all the way to the surface.

5. Begin by stitching two or three stitches in place (drop feed dogs or set stitch length at 0), or use your machine's lock stitch feature, if equipped, to anchor thread. Return setting to selected Blanket Stitch.

6. Most of the Blanket Stitch should be on the appliqué with the right edges of the stitch falling at the very outside edge of the appliqué. Stitch over all exposed raw edges of appliqué pieces.

7. (Note: Dots on ***Figs. 22 – 26*** indicate where to leave needle in fabric when pivoting.) Always stopping with needle down in background fabric, refer to ***Fig. 22*** to stitch outside points like tips of leaves. Stop one stitch short of point. Raise presser foot. Pivot project slightly, lower presser foot, and make an angled Stitch 1. Take next stitch, stop at point, and pivot so Stitch 2 will be perpendicular to point. Pivot slightly to make Stitch 3. Continue stitching.

Fig. 22

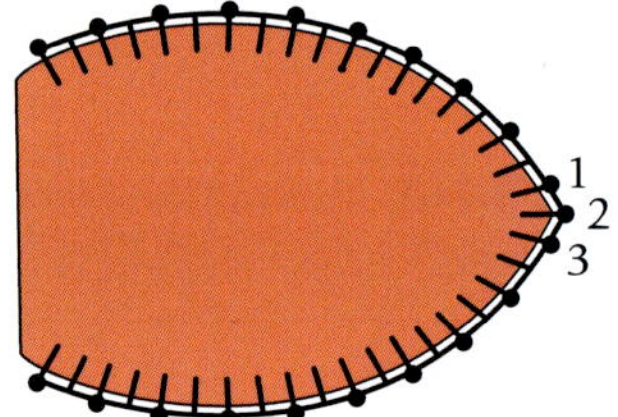

8. For outside corners ***(Fig. 23)***, stitch to corner, stopping with needle in background fabric. Raise presser foot. Pivot project, lower presser foot, and take an angled stitch. Raise presser foot. Pivot project, lower presser foot and stitch adjacent side.

Fig. 23

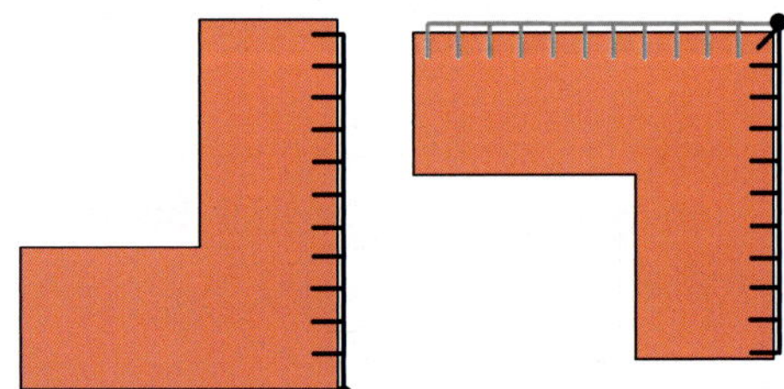

9. For inside corners *(Fig. 24)*, stitch to the corner, taking the last bite at corner and stopping with the needle down in background fabric. Raise presser foot. Pivot project, lower presser foot, and take an angled stitch. Raise presser foot. Pivot project, lower presser foot and stitch adjacent side.

Fig. 24

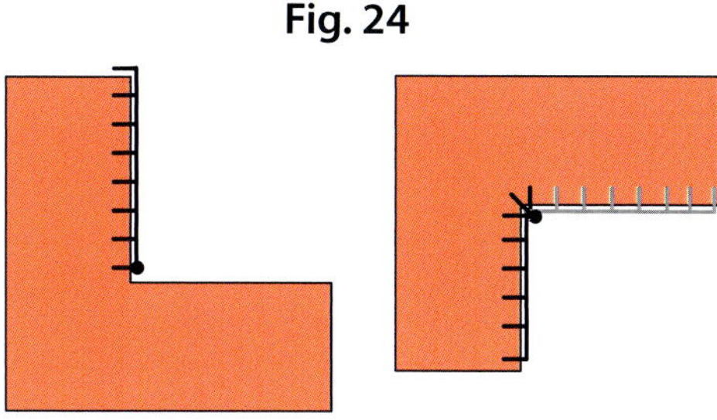

10. When stitching outside curves *(Fig. 25)*, stop with needle down in background fabric. Raise presser foot and pivot project as needed. Lower presser foot and continue stitching, pivoting as often as necessary to follow curve. Small circles may require pivoting between each stitch.

Fig. 25

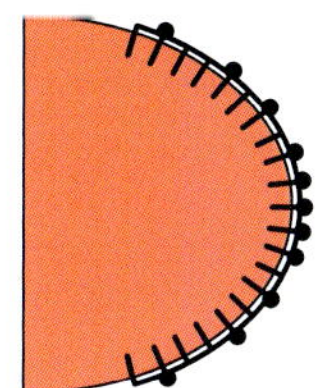

11. When stitching inside curves *(Fig. 26)*, stop with needle down in background fabric. Raise presser foot and pivot project as needed. Lower presser foot and continue stitching, pivoting as often as necessary to follow curve.

Fig. 26

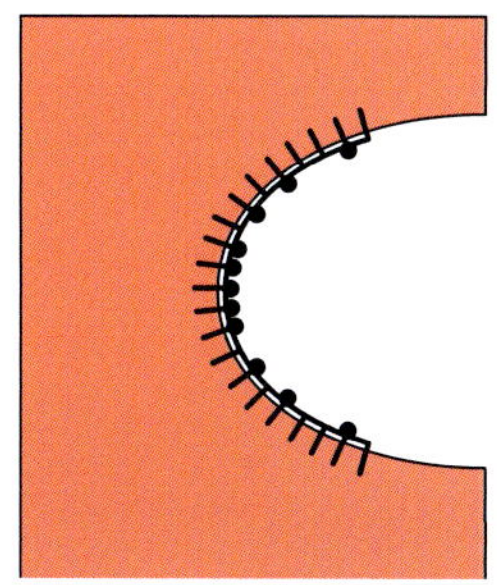

12. When stopping stitching, use a lock stitch to sew 5 or 6 stitches in place or use a needle to pull threads to wrong side of background fabric *(Fig. 27)*; knot, then trim ends.

Fig. 27

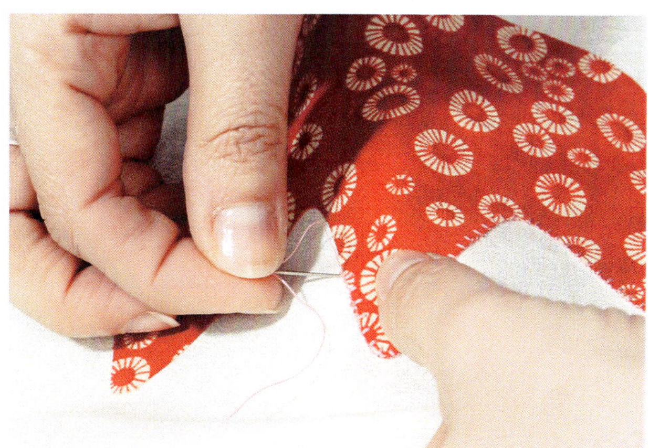

13. Carefully tear away stabilizer, if used.

BORDERS

ADDING SQUARED BORDERS

In most cases, our instructions for cutting borders for bed-size quilts include an extra 2" of length at each end for "insurance;" borders will be trimmed after measuring completed center section of quilt top.

1. Mark the center of each edge of quilt top.

2. Squared borders are usually added to sides, then top and bottom edges of the quilt top center. To add side borders, lay quilt top center on a flat surface; measure across quilt top center to determine length of borders ***(Fig. 28)***. Trim side borders to the determined length.

3. Mark center of 1 long edge of side border. Matching center marks and raw edges, pin border to quilt top, easing in any fullness; stitch. Press seam allowances toward the border.

4. Measure across center of quilt top, including attached borders, to determine length of top and bottom borders ***(Fig. 29)***. Trim top/bottom borders to the determined length. Repeat Step 3 to add borders to quilt top.

Fig. 28 **Fig. 29**

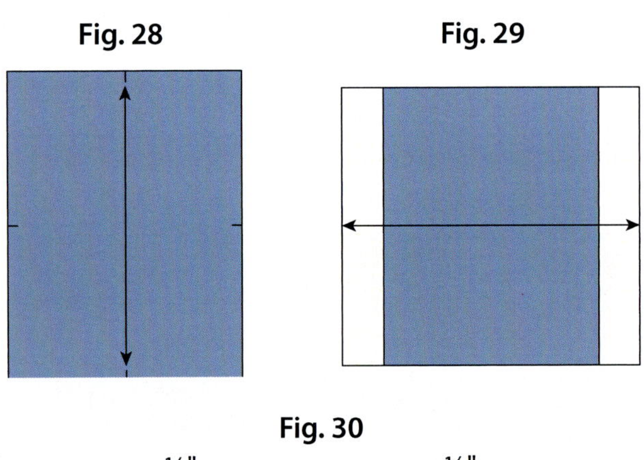

Fig. 30

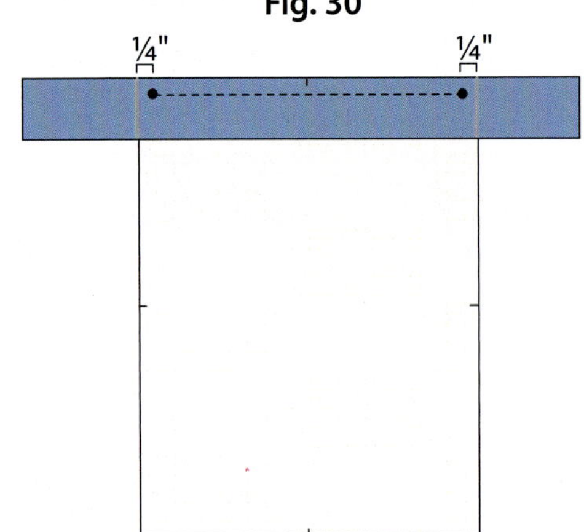

ADDING MITERED BORDERS

1. Mark the center of each edge of quilt top.

2. Mark center of 1 long edge of top border. Measure across center of quilt top ***(see Fig. 28)***. Matching center marks and raw edges, pin border to center of quilt top edge. From center of border, measure out ½ the width of the quilt top in both directions and mark. Match marks on border with corners of quilt top and pin. Easing in any fullness, pin border to quilt top between center and corners. Sew border to quilt top, beginning and ending seams exactly ¼" from each corner of quilt top and backstitching at beginning and end of stitching ***(Fig. 30)***.

3. Repeat Step 2 to sew botom, then side borders, to center section of quilt top. To temporarily move first 2 borders out of the way, fold and pin ends as shown in **Fig. 31**.

4. Fold 1 corner of quilt top diagonally with right sides together; use rotary cutting ruler to mark stitching line as shown in **Fig. 32**. Pin strips together along drawn line. Sew on drawn line, backstitching at beginning and end of stitching ***(Fig. 33)***.

5. Turn mitered corner right side up. Check to see that there is not a gap at the inner end of the seam and that corner does not pucker.

Fig. 31

Fig. 32

Fig. 33

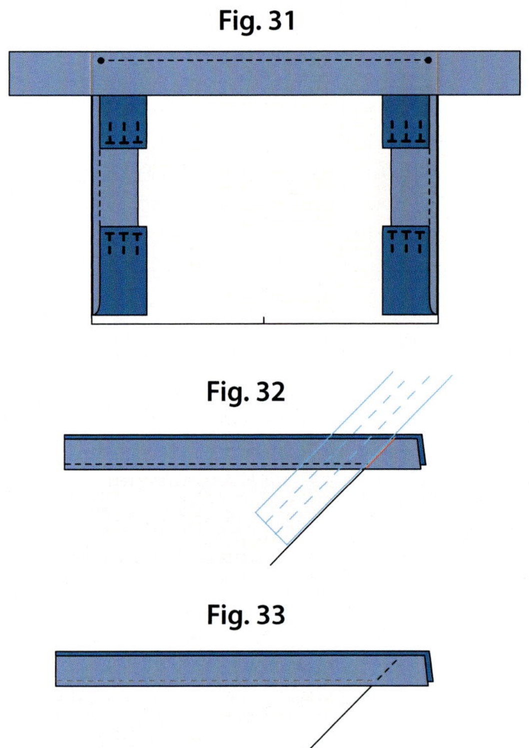

6. Trim seam allowances to ¼"; press to 1 side.

7. Repeat Steps 4-6 to miter each remaining corner.

QUILTING

Quilting holds the three layers (top, batting, and backing) of the quilt together and can be done by hand or machine. Because marking, layering, and quilting are interrelated and may be done in different orders depending on circumstances, please read entire Quilting section, pages 63 – 64, before beginning project.

TYPES OF QUILTING DESIGNS

In the Ditch Quilting

Quilting along seamlines or along edges of appliquéd pieces is called "in the ditch" quilting. This type of quilting should be done on side opposite seam allowance and does not have to be marked.

Outline Quilting

Quilting a consistent distance, usually ¼", from seam or appliqué is called "outline" quilting. Outline quilting may be marked, or ¼" wide masking tape may be placed along seamlines for quilting guide. (Do not leave tape on quilt longer than necessary, since it may leave an adhesive residue.)

Motif Quilting

Quilting a design, such as a feathered wreath, is called "motif" quilting. This type of quilting should be marked before basting quilt layers together.

Echo Quilting

Quilting that follows the outline of an appliquéd or pieced design with two or more parallel lines is called "echo" quilting. This type of quilting does not need to be marked.

Channel Quilting

Quilting with straight, parallel lines is called "channel" quilting. This type of quilting may be marked or stitched using a guide.

Crosshatch Quilting

Quilting straight lines in a grid pattern is called "crosshatch" quilting. Lines may be stitched parallel to edges of quilt or stitched diagonally. This type of quilting may be marked or stitched using a guide.

Meandering Quilting

Quilting in random curved lines and swirls is called "meandering" quilting. Quilting lines should not cross or touch each other. This type of quilting does not need to be marked.

Stipple Quilting

Meandering quilting that is very closely spaced is called "stipple" quilting. Stippling will flatten the area quilted and is often stitched in background areas to raise appliquéd or pieced designs. This type of quilting does not need to be marked.

MARKING QUILTING LINES

Quilting lines may be marked using fabric marking pencils, chalk markers, water- or air-soluble pens.

Simple quilting designs may be marked with chalk or chalk pencil after basting. A small area may be marked, then quilted, before moving to next area to be marked. Intricate designs should be marked before basting using a more durable marker.

Caution: Pressing may permanently set some marks. Test different markers on scrap fabric to find one that marks clearly and can be thoroughly removed.

A wide variety of pre-cut quilting stencils, as well as entire books of quilting patterns, are available. Using a stencil makes it easier to mark intricate or repetitive designs.

To make a stencil from a pattern, center template plastic over pattern and use a permanent marker to trace pattern onto plastic. Use a craft knife with single or double blade to cut channels along traced lines ***(Fig. 34)***.

Fig. 34

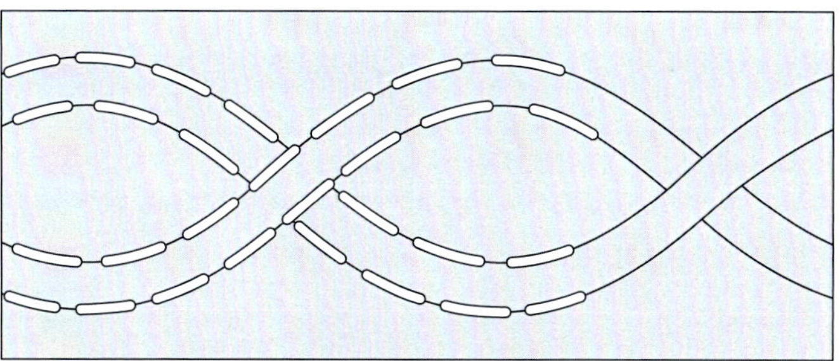

PREPARING THE BACKING

To allow for slight shifting of quilt top during quilting, backing should be approximately 4" larger on all sides. Yardage requirements listed for quilt backings are calculated for 43"/44"w fabric. Using 90"w or 108"w fabric for the backing of a bed-sized quilt may eliminate piecing. To piece a backing using 43"/44"w fabric, use the following instructions.

1. Measure length and width of quilt top; add 8" to each measurement.

2. If determined width is 79" or less, cut backing fabric into two lengths slightly longer than determined length measurement. Trim selvages. Place lengths with right sides facing and sew long edges together, forming tube ***(Fig. 35)***. Match seams and press along one fold ***(Fig. 36)***. Cut along pressed fold to form single piece (Fig. 37).

Fig. 35 **Fig. 36** **Fig. 37**

3. If determined width is more than 79", it may require less fabric yardage if the backing is pieced horizontally. Divide determined length measurement by 40" to determine how many widths will be needed. Cut required number of widths the determined width measurement. Trim selvages. Sew long edges together to form single piece.

4. Trim backing to size determined in Step 1; press seam allowances open.

CHOOSING THE BATTING

The appropriate batting will make quilting easier. For fine hand quilting, choose low-loft batting. All cotton or cotton/polyester blend battings work well for machine quilting because the cotton helps "grip" quilt layers. If quilt is to be tied, a high-loft batting, sometimes called extra-loft or fat batting, may be used to make quilt "fluffy."

Types of batting include cotton, polyester, wool, cotton/polyester blend, cotton/wool blend, and silk.

When selecting batting, refer to package labels for characteristics and care instructions. Cut batting same size as prepared backing.

ASSEMBLING THE QUILT

1. Examine wrong side of quilt top closely; trim any seam allowances and clip any threads that may show through front of the quilt. Press quilt top, being careful not to "set" any marked quilting lines.

2. Place backing wrong side up on flat surface. Use masking tape to tape edges of backing to surface. Place batting on top of backing fabric. Smooth batting gently, being careful not to stretch or tear. Center quilt top right side up on batting.

3. If machine quilting, use 1" rustproof safety pins to "pin-baste" all layers together, spacing pins approximately 4" apart. Begin at center and work toward outer edges to secure all layers. If possible, place pins away from areas that will be quilted, although pins may be removed as needed when quilting.

MACHINE QUILTING METHODS

Use general-purpose thread in bobbin. Do not use quilting thread. Thread the needle of machine with general-purpose thread or transparent monofilament thread to make quilting blend with quilt top fabrics. Use decorative thread, such as a metallic or contrasting-color general-purpose thread, to make quilting lines stand out more.

STRAIGHT-LINE QUILTING

The term "straight-line" is somewhat deceptive, since curves (especially gentle ones) as well as straight lines can be stitched with this technique.

1. Set stitch length for six to ten stitches per inch and attach walking foot to sewing machine.

2. Determine which section of quilt will have longest continuous quilting line, oftentimes area from center top to center bottom. Roll up and secure each edge of quilt to help reduce the bulk, keeping fabrics smooth. Smaller projects may not need to be rolled.

3. Begin stitching on longest quilting line, using very short stitches for the first ¼" to "lock" quilting. Stitch across project, using one hand on each side of walking foot to slightly spread fabric and to guide fabric through machine. Lock stitches at end of quilting line.

4. Continue machine quilting, stitching longer quilting lines first to stabilize quilt before moving on to other areas.

FREE-MOTION QUILTING

Free-motion quilting may be free form or may follow a marked pattern.

1. Attach darning foot to sewing machine and lower or cover feed dogs.

2. Position quilt under darning foot; lower foot. Holding top thread, take a stitch and pull bobbin thread to top of quilt. To "lock" beginning of quilting line, hold top and bobbin threads while making three to five stitches in place.

3. Use one hand on each side of darning foot to slightly spread fabric and to move fabric through the machine. Even stitch length is achieved by using smooth, flowing hand motion and steady machine speed. Slow machine speed and fast hand movement will create long stitches. Fast machine speed and slow hand movement will create short stitches. Move quilt sideways, back and forth, in a circular motion, or in a random motion to create desired designs; do not rotate quilt. Lock stitches at end of each quilting line.

MAKING A HANGING SLEEVE

Attaching a hanging sleeve to back of wall hanging or quilt before the binding is added allows project to be displayed on wall.

1. Measure width of quilt top edge and subtract 1". Cut piece of fabric 7"w by determined measurement.

2. Press short edges of fabric piece ¼" to wrong side; press edges ¼" to wrong side again and machine stitch in place.

3. Matching wrong sides, fold piece in half lengthwise to form tube.

4. Follow project instructions to sew binding to quilt top and to trim backing and batting. Before Blindstitching binding to backing, match raw edges and stitch hanging sleeve to center top edge on back of quilt.

5. Finish binding quilt, treating hanging sleeve as part of backing.

6. Blindstitch bottom of hanging sleeve to backing, taking care not to stitch through to front of quilt.

7. Insert dowel or slat into hanging sleeve.

MAKING A CONTINUOUS BIAS STRIP

Bias strips for binding or appliqué can simply be cut and pieced to desired length. However, when a long length of binding is needed, the "continuous" method is quick and accurate.

1. Use square cut from binding fabric called for in project instructions. Cut square in half diagonally to make two triangles.

2. With right sides together and using ¼" seam allowance, sew triangles together ***(Fig. 38)***; press seam allowances open.

Fig. 38

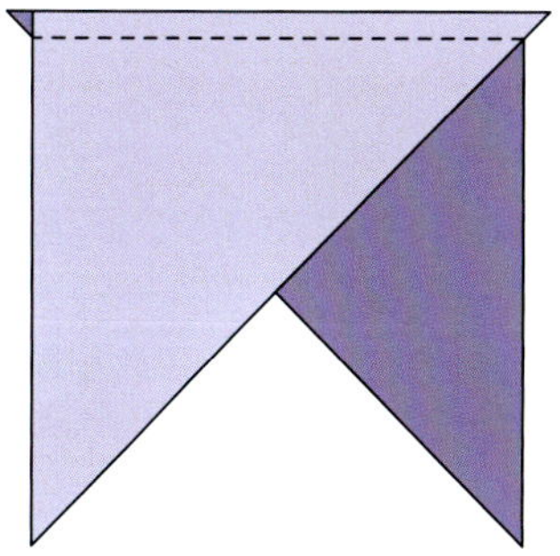

3. On wrong side of fabric, draw lines the width of binding as specified in project instructions ***(Fig. 39)***. Cut off any remaining fabric less than this width.

Fig. 39

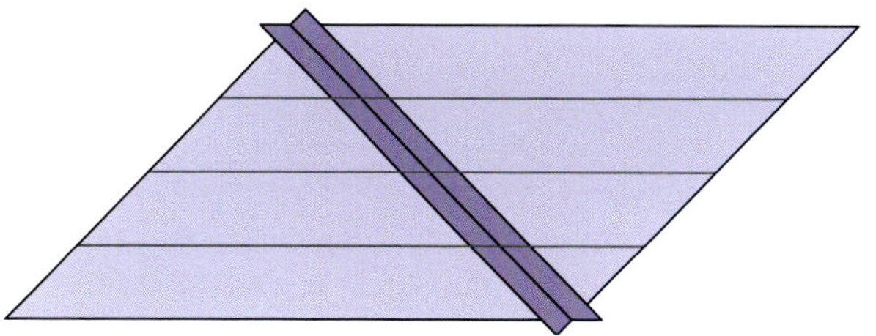

4. With right sides inside, bring short edges together to form tube; match raw edges so that first drawn line of top section meets second drawn line of bottom section ***(Fig. 40)***.

Fig. 40

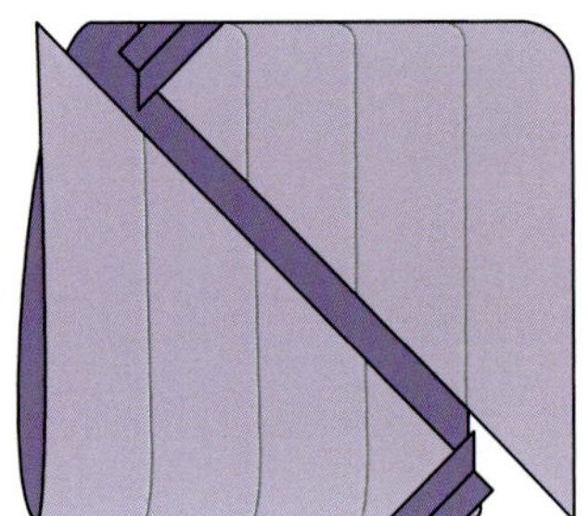

5. Carefully pin edges together by inserting pins through drawn lines at point where drawn lines intersect, making sure pins go through intersections on both sides. Using ¼" seam allowance, sew edges together; press seam allowances open.

6. To cut continuous strip, begin cutting along first drawn line ***(Fig. 41)***. Continue cutting along drawn line around tube.

Fig. 41

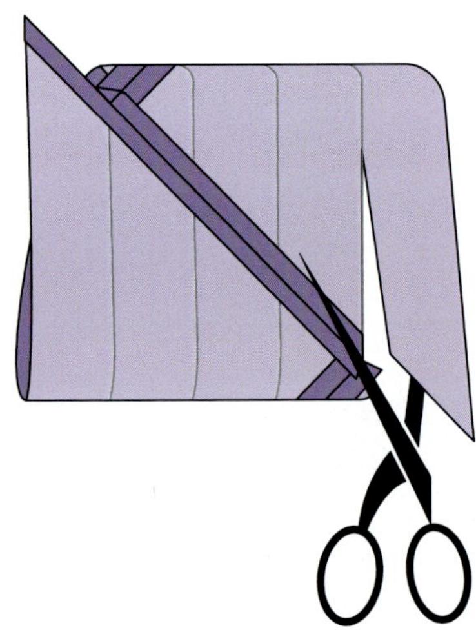

7. Trim ends of bias strip square.

ATTACHING BINDING WITH MITERED CORNERS

1. Matching wrong sides and raw edges, press continuous strip in half lengthwise to complete binding.

2. Beginning with one end near center on bottom edge of quilt, lay binding around quilt to make sure that seams in binding will not end up at a corner. Adjust placement if necessary. Matching raw edges of binding to raw edge of quilt top, pin binding to right side of quilt along one edge.

3. When you reach first corner, mark ¼" from corner of quilt top ***(Fig. 42)***.

Fig. 42

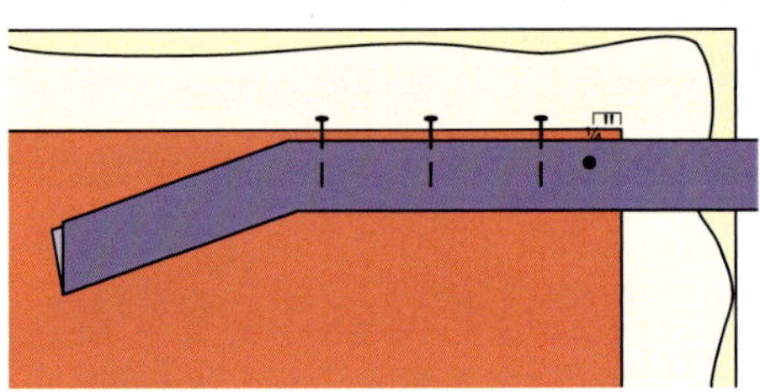

4. Beginning approximately 10" from end of binding and using ¼" seam allowance, sew binding to quilt, backstitching at beginning of stitching and at mark ***(Fig. 43)***. Lift needle out of fabric and clip thread.

Fig. 43

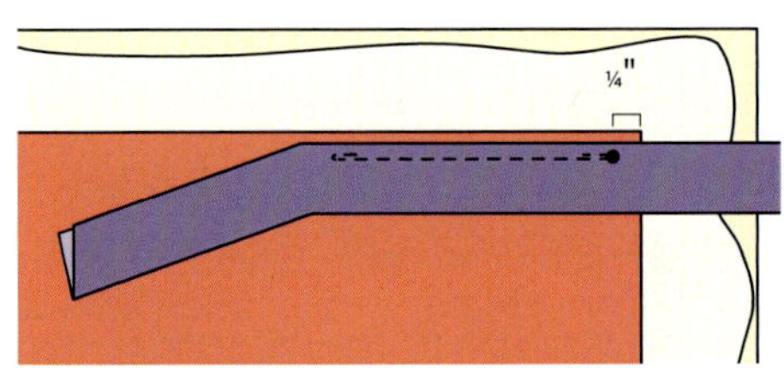

5. Fold binding as shown in ***Figs. 44 – 45*** and pin binding to adjacent side, matching raw edges. When you've reached the next corner, mark ¼" from edge of quilt top.

Fig. 44

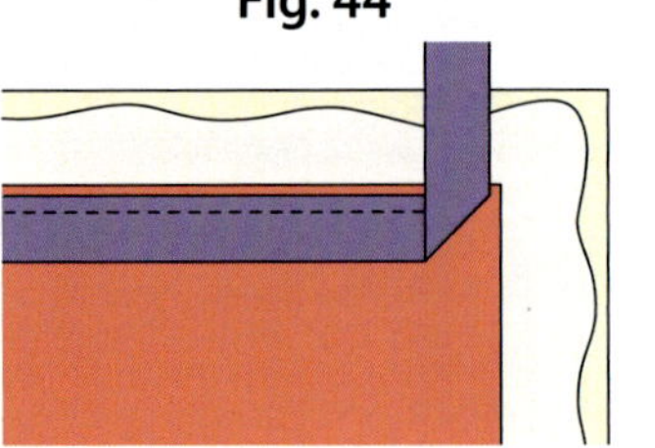

Fig. 45

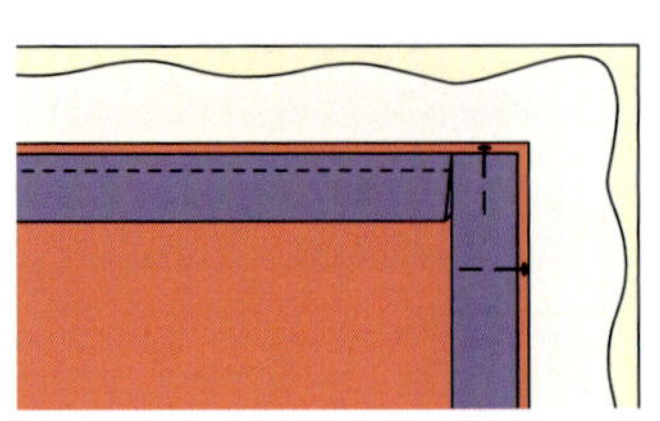

6. Backstitching at edge of quilt top, sew pinned binding to quilt ***(Fig. 46)***; backstitch at the next mark. Lift needle out of fabric and clip thread.

Fig. 46

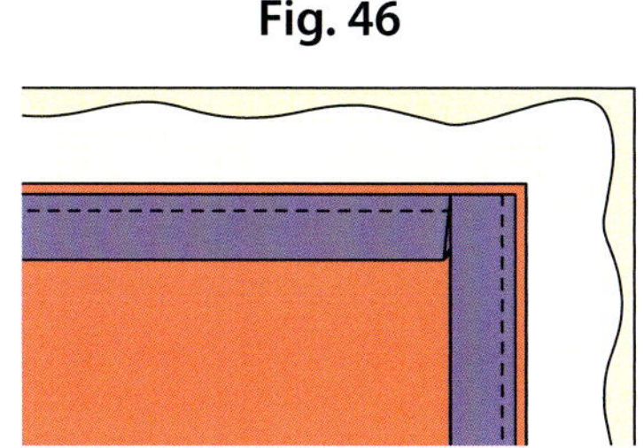

7. Continue sewing binding to quilt, stopping approximately 10" from starting point ***(Fig. 47)***.

Fig. 47

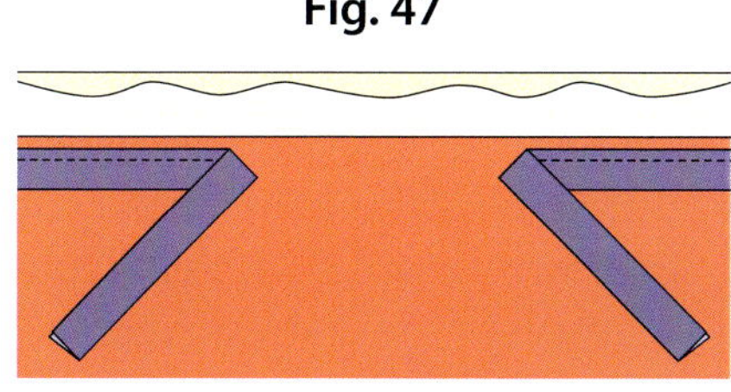

8. Bring beginning and end of binding to center of opening and fold each end back, leaving a ¼" space between folds ***(Fig. 48)***. Finger press folds.

Fig. 48

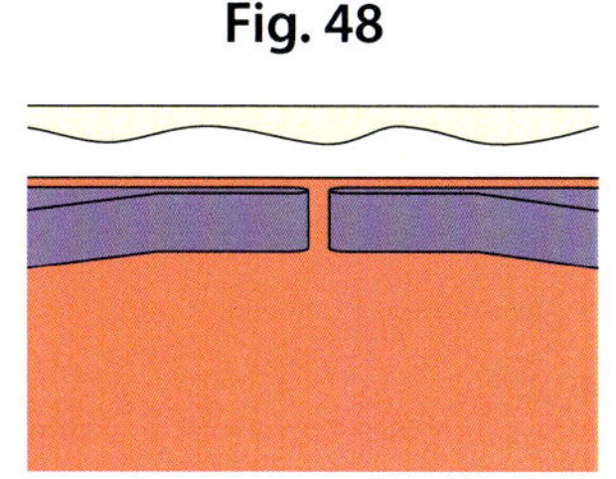

9. Unfold ends of binding and draw a line across wrong side in finger-pressed crease. Draw a line through the lengthwise pressed fold of binding at the same spot to create a cross mark. With edge of ruler at cross mark, line up 45° angle marking on ruler with one long side of binding. Draw a diagonal line from edge to edge. Repeat on remaining end, making sure that the two diagonal lines are angled the same way ***(Fig. 49)***

Fig. 49

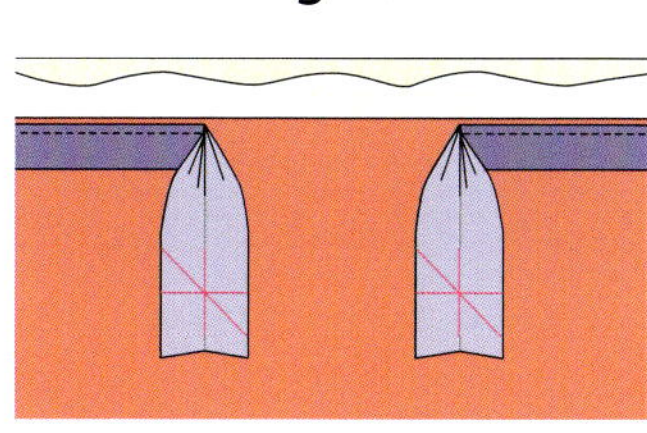

10. Matching right sides and diagonal lines, pin binding ends together at right angles ***(Fig. 50)***.

Fig. 50

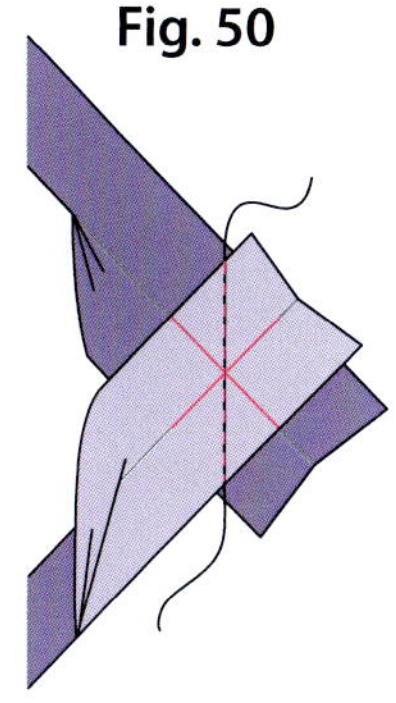

11. Machine stitch along diagonal line ***(Fig. 51)***, removing pins as you stitch.

Fig. 51

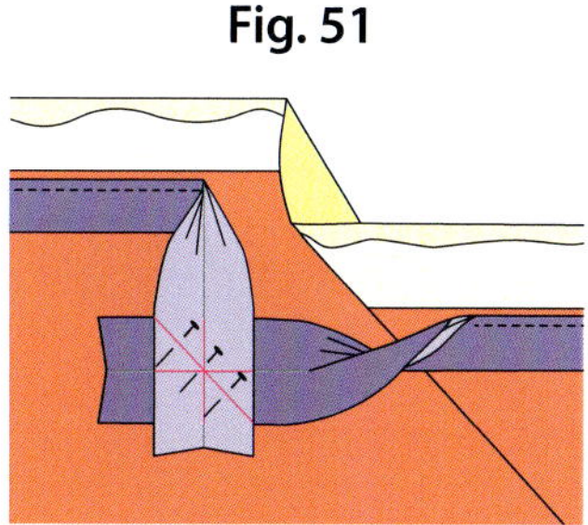

12. Lay binding against quilt to double check that it is correct length.

13. Trim binding ends, leaving ¼" seam allowance; press seam open. Stitch binding to quilt.

14. If using 2½"w binding (finished size ½"), trim backing and batting a scant ¼" larger than quilt top so that batting and backing will fill the binding when it is folded over to quilt backing. If using narrower binding, trim backing and batting even with edges of quilt top.

15. On one edge of quilt, fold binding over to quilt backing and pin pressed edge in place, covering stitching line ***(Fig. 52)***. On adjacent side, fold binding over, forming a mitered corner ***(Fig. 53)***. Repeat to pin remainder of binding in place.

Fig. 52 **Fig. 53**

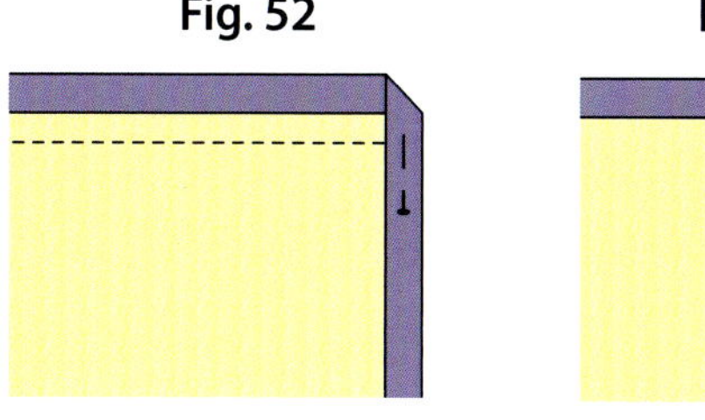

16. Blindstitch binding to backing, taking care not to stitch through to front of quilt.

BLIND STITCH

Come up at 1, go down at 2, and come up at 3 ***(Fig. 54)***. Length of stitches may be varied as desired.

Fig. 54

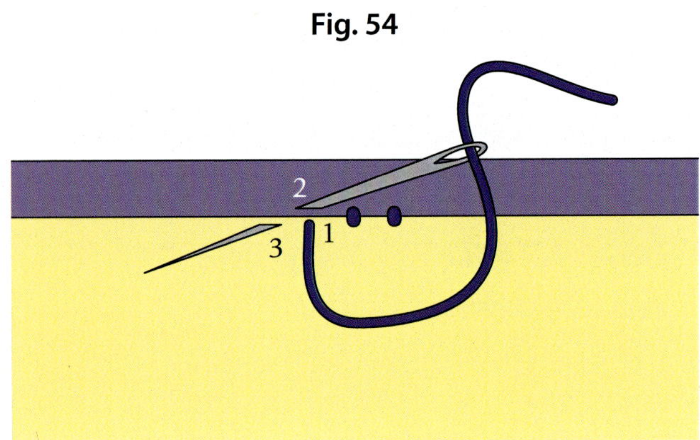

SIGNING AND DATING YOUR QUILT

A completed quilt is a work of art and should be signed and dated. There are many different ways to do this and numerous books on the subject. The label should reflect the style of the quilt, the occasion or person for which it was made, and the quilter's own particular talents. Following are suggestions for recording the history of quilt or adding a sentiment for future generations.

- Embroider quilter's name, date, and any additional information on quilt top or backing. Matching floss, such as cream floss on white border, will leave a subtle record. Bright or contrasting floss will make the information stand out.
- Make label from muslin and use permanent marker to write information. Use different colored permanent markers to make label more decorative. Stitch label to back of quilt.
- Use photo-transfer paper to add image to white or cream fabric label. Stitch label to back of quilt.
- Piece an extra block from quilt top pattern to use as label. Add information with permanent fabric pen. Appliqué block to back of quilt.
- Write message on appliquéd design from quilt top. Attach appliqué to back of the quilt.

Metric Conversion Chart

Inches x 2.54 = centimeters (cm)	Yards x .9144 = meters (m)
Inches x 25.4 = millimeters (mm)	Yards x 91.44 = centimeters (cm)
Inches x .0254 = meters (m)	Centimeters x .3937 = inches (")
	Meters x 1.0936 = yards (yd)

Standard Equivalents

1/8"	3.2 mm	0.32 cm	1/8 yard	11.43 cm	0.11 m
1/4"	6.35 mm	0.635 cm	1/4 yard	22.86 cm	0.23 m
3/8"	9.5 mm	0.95 cm	3/8 yard	34.29 cm	0.34 m
1/2"	12.7 mm	1.27 cm	1/2 yard	45.72 cm	0.46 m
5/8"	15.9 mm	1.59 cm	5/8 yard	57.15 cm	0.57 m
3/4"	19.1 mm	1.91 cm	3/4 yard	68.58 cm	0.69 m
7/8"	22.2 mm	2.22 cm	7/8 yard	80 cm	0.8 m
1"	25.4 mm	2.54 cm	1 yard	91.44 cm	0.91 m

Production Team: Technical Editor - Lisa Lancaster; Technical Associate Editor - Janie Wright; Graphic Artists - Christine Roa DeLillo & Zachary Kline;

Made in U.S.A.